Joshua

K.W. Bow

Copyright 2017 by Kenneth W. Bow
The book author retains sole copyright to
his contributions to this book.
Published 2017.
Printed in the United States of America.

All rights reserved.

No portion of this book may be reproduced, stored in a retrieval system, or transmitted in any form or by any means – electronic, mechanical, photocopy, recording, scanning, or other – except for brief quotations in critical reviews or articles, without the prior written permission of the author.

ISBN 978-1-946234-11-7

Cover art and design: Mark Gauthier.
Editor-in-chief: Susan Lind.

This book was published by BookCrafters,
Parker, Colorado.
bookcrafterscolorado@gmail.com

This book may be ordered from
www.bookcrafters.net and other online bookstores.

Foreword

Thank you reader, for selecting my book. There are many choices of books and we all have a limited window of time to read. I appreciate you purchasing my product. It is a humbling thing to know someone would choose to purchase, and then read your work. I do not take it as a small matter. By purchasing and reading a book, the reader and the author form a certain bond as they travel a road together for a short time. It is especially rewarding when the two agree on the content. It is my hope you can find inspiration and life challenges in the pages of this small booklet.

From the days of my high school years I have found the Bible fascinating. I have travelled to Israel on two occasions to learn more about the land and culture of the Bible. I worked on an archaeological dig and lived on a Kibbutz to better inform myself of how to understand this book from God. I have read it from cover to cover over twenty times, and it is still as exciting to me as it ever was.

The Bible is a magnificent journey and experience. It is ever a delight. In it you will travel to distant lands and meet some of the most incredible people of history. It will introduce you to kings and peasants. You will walk the palace halls of castles and the open fields of the countryside. You will meet the famous and be introduced to people whose name we will never know. You will read some of the greatest love stories ever told and you will see the dark side of man as the evil manifests itself in heinous ways. Every emotion of man is highlighted at some time. You will see greed and avarice and murderous covetousness. You will also see the greatest examples of love and sacrifice that mankind has ever contributed. For indeed the Bible is the story of man. It is the whole story, and nothing is left out or omitted. It is the ultimate mirror of life.

When we invest time in the Bible we indulge a bit of the eternal. The Bible will never pass away, even in the eons of the future. If you have read it sincerely then my hope is this small work will intensify your understanding and enjoyment a little more. It is the grandest journey we can make while in this life. Thank you for sharing a portion of your life journey with me.

Kenneth Bow

Introduction

The job of succeeding the greatest law given in history would not be a coveted one. Moses was dead. Now Joshua, the 28th from Adam is given the task to finish what Moses had started. Joshua had two main assignments. First, he was to lead military expeditions to conquer the land. Second, he was to divide the land for the inheritance of the tribes.

This book only covers about seven years of time. It is mainly a historical book, but the Bible never writes history for the sake of history itself. The underlying purpose is always divine purpose. This book is overwhelmingly positive. Israel met with unprecedented success. The book concludes with "there failed not aught for any good thing which the Lord had spoken unto the house of Israel; all came to pass." (21.45)

Standing beside the river about to invade the land, this same group of people had stood there forty years earlier. What had changed? In some ways not much had changed. On the other hand some things that mattered greatly had radically changed. The people in the wilderness wandering had been guilty of complaining and murmuring on numerous occasions. In this book there is no record of a single instance of rebellion or resistance to their leadership. That attitude shift was the single most important factor in their success or failure in the next seven years. The slave mentality of the previous generation was gone. This generation was born free and desert bred.

This ragtag army of sorts had no chariots or horses. They had primitive weapons of war at best. They had a new untested leader who would make some serious mistakes. But they had one indispensable element. They had faith in God, and that swung the result in their favor. They fought unconventionally. The world had never seen an army quite like this before. They spent their first week in the new land performing circumcision on their children and observing religious rituals. They built a stone monument to God.

When they begin the actual assault it seems bizarre to the inhabitants of Jericho. The truth was they were allowing God to direct their every move, and this was the secret to their improbable success. The dismal, doubting, attitude of the previous generation was buried with their remains somewhere in the Sinai desert. This generation was ready to listen to every nuance of God's direction.

Listen they did, and the rest is history. This untrained, ill equipped mass of people conquered their promised land in seven years. A nation was born that would thrive and grow from a rural people to an urban people, and finally take their place among the nations of the world. God had extracted slaves from mighty Egypt as the raw material to formulate His special people and their homeland. In the next millennium this nation would scale the summit of the world and build the grandest building the world had ever seen.

The book of Joshua proves the summit is reached by listening to God and obeying His commands. Superior weapons of war will never trump simple obedience.

Author: Uncertain, possibly Joshua.

Date: 1400 BC

Theme: The secret of conquering Promised Land.

Chapter 1

1.1-2 Now after the death of Moses the servant of the Lord it came to pass, that the Lord spake unto Joshua the son of Nun, Moses' minister, saying, 2 Moses my servant is dead; now therefore arise, go over this Jordan, thou, and all this people, unto the land which I do give to them, even to the children of Israel.

1.1-2 Moses is dead. Joshua was Moses' assistant and military field commander. He had been a spiritual disciple as well. He had accompanied Moses up the mountain to receive the law at Sinai. He had also been one of two sent to evaluate the land forty years before and returned with a positive report. One of his truly great attributes was his simple faith. His faith became the canopy of the new nation. Joshua's abilities were revealed by his administration and military genius. At the end of Joshua's life he also died with unfinished tasks he set out to do, just as Moses did.

1.3-9 Every place that the sole of your foot shall tread upon, that have I given unto you, as I said unto Moses. 4 From the wilderness and this Lebanon even unto the great river, the river Euphrates, all the land of the Hittites, and unto the great sea toward the going down of the sun, shall be your coast. 5 There shall not any man

be able to stand before thee all the days of thy life: as I was with Moses, so I will be with thee: I will not fail thee, nor forsake thee. 6 Be strong and of a good courage: for unto this people shalt thou divide for an inheritance the land, which I sware unto their fathers to give them. 7 Only be thou strong and very courageous, that thou mayest observe to do according to all the law, which Moses my servant commanded thee: turn not from it to the right hand or to the left, that thou mayest prosper withersoever thou goest. 8 This book of the law shall not depart out of thy mouth; but thou shalt meditate therein day and night, that thou mayest observe to do according to all that is written therein: for then thou shalt make thy way prosperous, and then thou shalt have good success. 9 Have not I commanded thee? Be strong and of a good courage; be not afraid, neither be thou dismayed: for the Lord thy God is with thee whithersoever thou goest.

1.3-9 The promise renewed. The promise spoken to Moses is renewed to Joshua. In the midst of a change in leadership there is no change in the promise. This is an eternal principal in God. Their success is anchored in the book of the law. At the outset of the formation of the nation, God is setting some principals in motion to guide the nation. Complete obedience is essential. Adherence to the letter of the law is mandatory. These principals will always bring success. Prosperity and success come packaged in complete, exact obedience. This lesson will be driven home vividly by the issue with Achan.

1.10-18 Then Joshua commanded the officers of the people, saying, 11 Pass through the host, and command the people, saying, Prepare you victuals; for within three days ye shall pass over this Jordan, to go in to possess the land, which the Lord your God giveth you to possess

it. **12 And to the Reubenites, and to the Gadites, and to half the tribe of Manasseh, spake Joshua, saying, 13 Remember the word which Moses the servant of the Lord commanded you, saying, The Lord your God hath given you rest, and hath given you this land. 14 Your wives, your little ones, and your cattle, shall remain in the land which Moses gave you on this side Jordan; but ye shall pass before your brethren armed, all the mighty men of valour, and help them; 15 Until the Lord have given your brethren rest, as he hath given you, and they also have possessed the land which the Lord your God giveth them: then ye shall return unto the land of your possession, and enjoy it, which Moses the Lord's servant gave you on this side Jordan toward the sunrising. 16 And they answered Joshua, saying, All that thou commandest us we will do, and whithersoever thou sendest us, we will go. 17 According as we hearkened unto Moses in all things, so will we hearken unto thee: only the Lord thy God be with thee, as he was with Moses. 18 Whosoever he be that doth rebel against thy commandment, and will not hearken unto thy words in all that thou commandest him, he shall be put to death: only be strong and of a good courage.**

1.10-18 The people respond. Joshua assumes command. He notifies that in three days they will begin. The people pledge loyalty and fidelity. They agree that if any rebel against Joshua, the penalty is death. This unified disposition will galvanize this untrained army into a cohesive unit that sweeps through the land in unprecedented military conquest. To the outward man this must look like an unorganized mass of men with no plan. In truth, they were the agents of God, and God had a perfect plan. One must pause to ponder the three days. This period of time is a recognized time in the Bible of death and finality. Were they burying their desert journey? Were they bidding adieu to any return to the wilderness? Looking across the river at Jericho, maybe they needed this final funeral of the past to jump-start the process of war. The people prepare, then pass over and finally possess the promise (11). This is an eternal allegory. The people of God universally in every age, prepare (salvation), then pass over (coming of the Lord), then possess the promise (heaven).

Chapter 2

2.1-2 And Joshua the son of Nun sent out of Shittim two men to spy secretly, saying, Go view the land, even Jericho. And they went, and came into an harlot's house, named Rahab, and lodged there. 2 And it was told the king of Jericho, saying, Behold, there came men in hither to night of the children of Israel to search out the country.

2.1-2 Shittim. This had been a place of failure (Num 25.1-13), but now becomes the invasion point of victory. The underlying message here is that defeat is not final. Past failures do not limit our future. In the incident in Numbers 25, 24,000 people died before Phineas aborted the plague. Josephus places Shittim seven miles from the Jordan River. The two emissaries of Joshua arrived in Jericho and went to Rahab's house. Rahab was a harlot of Jericho. She believed the God of Israel was the true God. She manifests actions that are wrong like lying and immorality, but shows mercy to the spies. For this her life and the life of her family is spared. She will eventually marry Salmon who was the father of Boaz, the man who Ruth marries and was the ancestor of King David. Thus Rahab became the ancestress of Jesus Christ by her de facto faith.

2.3-15 And the king of Jericho sent unto Rahab, saying, Bring forth the men that are come to thee, which are entered into thine house: for they be come to search out all the country. 4 And the woman took the two men, and hid them, and said thus, There came men unto me, but I wist not whence they were: 5 And it came to pass about the time of shutting of the gate, when it was dark, that the men went out: whither the men went I wot not: pursue after them quickly; for ye shall overtake them. 6 But she had brought them up to the roof of the house, and hid them with the stalks of flax, which she had laid in order upon the roof. 7 And the men pursued after them the way to Jordan unto the fords: and as soon as they which pursued after them were gone out, they shut the gate. 8 And before they were laid down, she came up unto them upon the roof; 9 And she said unto the men, I know that the Lord hath given you the land, and that your terror is fallen upon us, and that all the inhabitants of the land faint because of you. 10 For we have heard how the Lord dried up the water of the Red sea for you, when ye came out of Egypt; and what ye did unto the two kings of the Amorites, that were on the other side Jordan, Sihon and Og, whom ye utterly destroyed. 11 And as soon as we had heard these things, our hearts did melt, neither did there remain any more courage in any man, because of you: for the Lord your God, he is God in heaven above, and in earth beneath. 12 Now therefore, I pray you, swear unto me by the Lord, since I have shewed you kindness, that ye will also shew kindness unto my father's house, and give me a true token: 13 And that ye will save alive my father, and my mother, and my brethren, and my sisters, and all that they have, and deliver our lives from death. 14 And the men answered her, Our life for yours, if ye utter not this our business. And it shall be, when the Lord hath given us the land, that we will deal kindly and truly with thee. 15 Then she let them down by a cord through the window: for her house was upon the town wall, and she dwelt upon the wall.

2.3-15 Spies and lies. Rahab hides the spies and then lies about it to the king. The ruse works and the spies escape safely. Rahab makes a secret pact to insure her survival. Her house on the wall was favored by harlots so men could come and go with minimal exposure to the inner city. She allowed the spies to escape out the window on the outer wall as other men did who visited her. Excavations in 1907-1909 discovered these same walls and houses intact.

2.16-24 And she said unto them, Get you to the mountain, lest the pursuers meet you; and hide yourselves there three days, until the pursuers be returned: and afterward may ye go your way. 17 And the men said unto her, We will be blameless of this thine oath which thou hast made us swear. 18 Behold, when we come into the land, thou shalt bind this line of scarlet thread in the window which thou didst let us down by: and thou shalt bring thy father, and thy mother, and thy brethren, and all thy father's household, home unto thee. 19 And it shall be, that whosoever shall go out of the doors of thy house into the street, his blood shall be upon his head, and we will be guiltless: and whosoever shall be with thee in the house, his blood shall be on our head, if any hand be upon him. 20 And if thou utter this our business, then we will be quit of thine oath which thou hast made us to swear. 21 And she said, According unto your words, so be it. And she sent them away, and they departed: and she bound the scarlet line in the window. 22 And they went, and came unto the mountain, and abode there three days, until the pursuers were returned: and the pursuers sought them throughout all the way, but found them

not. 23 So the two men returned, and descended from the mountain, and passed over, and came to Joshua the son of Nun, and told him all things that befell them: 24 And they said unto Joshua, Truly the Lord hath delivered into our hands all the land; for even all the inhabitants of the country do faint because of us.

2.16-24 The scarlet cord. The symbol of deliverance and covenant. The scarlet cord came to represent the blood of Jesus Christ, which brought salvation to a condemned world. It is through Christ's blood we escape the coming judgment. Christ's blood provides deliverance and protection to those under it's protection. It is of note that her family members were safe only as long as they were in the house protected by the scarlet cord. So the analogy is also true, only those under the blood of Jesus are safe from coming judgment. The spies fled to the mountains. The range of mountains near Jericho are called Quarantania and are honeycombed with many caves. This provided the spies concealment until they returned to Joshua.

Chapter 3

3.1-5 And Joshua rose early in the morning; and they removed from Shittim, and came to Jordan, he and all the children of Israel, and lodged there before they passed over. 2 And it came to pass after three days, that the officers went through the host; 3 And they commanded the people, saying, When ye see the ark of the covenant of the Lord your God, and the priests the Levites bearing it, then ye shall remove from your place, and go after it. 4 Yet there shall be a space between you and it, about two thousand cubits by measure: come not near unto it, that ye may know the way by which ye must go: for ye have not passed this way heretofore. 5 And Joshua said unto the people, Sanctify yourselves: for to morrow the Lord will do wonders among you.

3.1-5 Crossing the Jordan. Joshua was an early riser much like Jesus would be (6.12, 7.16, 8.10). The people journeyed the seven miles to the river and paused again for 3 days. The command to follow the Ark of the Covenant is symbolic. They were not to move until the ark led the way. They were required to keep about one half-mile distance away form the ark. God was giving lucid instructions to follow where and how He would lead them.

3.6-13 And Joshua spake unto the priests, saying, Take up the ark of the covenant, and pass over before the people. And they took up the ark of the covenant, and went before the people. 7 And the Lord said unto Joshua, This day will I begin to magnify thee in the sight of all Israel, that they may know that, as I was with Moses, so I will be with thee. 8 And thou shalt command the priests that bear the ark of the covenant, saying, When ye are come to the brink of the water of Jordan, ye shall stand still in Jordan. 9 And Joshua said unto the children of Israel, Come hither, and hear the words of the Lord your God. 10 And Joshua said, Hereby ye shall know that the living God is among you, and that he will without fail drive out from before you the Canaanites, and the Hittites, and the Hivites, and the Perizzites, and the Girgashites, and the Amorites, and the Jebusites. 11 Behold, the ark of the covenant of the Lord of all the earth passeth over before you into Jordan. 12 Now therefore take you twelve men out of the tribes of Israel, out of every tribe a man. 13 And it shall come to pass, as soon as the soles of the feet of the priests that bear the ark of the Lord, the Lord of all the earth, shall rest in the waters of Jordan, that the waters of Jordan shall be cut off from the waters that come down from above; and they shall stand upon an heap.

3.6-13 The miracle. God gives undeniable approbation to Joshua in the eyes of the people. The moment had arrived after forty years of anticipation. What feeling must had rippled through the tents of Israel as the priests hoisted the Ark of the Testament onto their shoulders. This was a once in a lifetime moment. To confirm His guiding voice to Joshua, Joshua proclaims the miraculous moment of the waters standing on heap. Carnal men always seek to downplay the miraculous. They want to ascribe this to an earthquake that dammed up the river or other such notions. The Bible clearly proclaims this was a divine act of God.

3.14-17 And it came to pass, when the people removed from their tents, to pass over Jordan, and the priests bearing the ark of the covenant before the people; 15 And as they that bare the ark were come unto Jordan, and the feet of the priests that bare the ark were dipped in the brim of the water, (for Jordan overfloweth all his banks all the time of harvest,) 16 That the waters which came down from above stood and rose up upon an heap very far from the city Adam, that is beside Zaretan: and those that came down toward the sea of the plain, even the salt sea, failed, and were cut off: and the people passed over right against Jericho. 17 And the priests that bare the ark of the covenant of the Lord stood firm on dry ground in the midst of Jordan, and all the Israelites passed over on dry ground, until all the people were passed clean over Jordan.

3.14-17 The water. Water is the most essential element of life along with oxygen. Water has played a significant role in the Bible. In creation the waters were separated in day two to form the atmosphere and the oceans. It was water that God used to destroy the antediluvian world by a flood. It was water that saved Moses' life. It was the lack of water that drove the patriarchs to Egypt during seasons of famine. Here in the crossing of the Jordan, God uses water to display His presence and His power. This is a foreshadowing of the power of water in the New Testament church. We find John the Baptist at the river baptizing. Jesus ministry is announced at the river with John. Jesus first miracle takes the element of water and turns it into wine. It is at a well of water Jesus reaches out to the woman of Samaria. Jesus heals at the pool of Bethesda. Jesus calms the storm on the waters of Galilee. The Apostle Paul makes the connection to the crossing through the water in the Old Testament to baptism in the New Testament. (1 Cor 10.1-2). When Nicodemus comes to Jesus and seeks how to be accepted in God, Jesus clearly speaks you must be born of water and spirit (Jn 3.1-7). This is accomplished in water baptism in the New Testament. Water baptism is proclaimed in every seismic shift of direction in the early church. It is the centerpiece of the first message in Acts 2. It is present in baptism when the door being opened to the Samaritans in Acts 8. It is required again in baptism when the gospel is taken to the gentiles for the first time in Acts 10. When the Apostle Paul is introduced to the disciples of John the Baptist in Acts 19, baptism is again the central issue. In Romans we are taught by Paul (Rom 6.4) that water represents the burial of the old man in the process of the New Birth by the death, the burial, and the resurrection. The water poured upon the ground by Moses that turned to blood was a beautiful type of the water of baptism that represents the blood of Jesus Christ that washes us from our sins. These desert born people were crossing through the water to the Promised Land. That is our template. We cross through the water of baptism to our promised land.

Chapter 4

4.1-7 And it came to pass, when all the people were clean passed over Jordan, that the Lord spake unto Joshua, saying, 2 Take you twelve men out of the people, out of every tribe a man, 3 And command ye them, saying, Take you hence out of the midst of Jordan, out of the place where the priests' feet stood firm, twelve stones, and ye shall carry them over with you, and leave them in the lodging place, where ye shall lodge this night. 4 Then Joshua called the twelve men, whom he had prepared of the children of Israel, out of every tribe a man: 5 And Joshua said unto them, Pass over before the ark of the Lord your God into the midst of Jordan, and take you up every man of you a stone upon his shoulder, according unto the number of the tribes of the children of Israel: 6 That this may be a sign among you, that when your children ask their fathers in time to come, saying, What mean ye by these stones? 7 Then ye shall answer them, That the waters of Jordan were cut off before the ark of the covenant of the Lord; when it passed over Jordan, the waters of Jordan were cut off: and these stones shall be for a memorial unto the children of Israel for ever.

4.1-7 The memorial. This moment was to be remembered. They were to build a memorial for future generations who had not been present when the miracle occurred. There was also a hidden memorial under the waters of the river unseen but still present. For this memorial, stones were used. The symbolism of stones is beautiful. Each stone is different. God would not allow any stone to be used in His altar that had been modified. (Ex 20.25). When the Tower of Babel was built they used bricks. Bricks represent man made. Everyone is the same. God creates stones, men create bricks. This memorial was about the unique people who had come through the desert trial, and now stood poised to fulfill a promise made to Abraham half a millennial before. These Israelites were not bricks, hand hewn by slavery, these Israelites were stones, uncut in their natural state and ready to fulfill their destiny.

4.8-11 And the children of Israel did so as Joshua commanded, and took up twelve stones out of the midst of Jordan, as the Lord spake unto Joshua, according to the number of the tribes of the children of Israel, and carried them over with them unto the place where they lodged, and laid them down there. 9 And Joshua set up twelve stones in the midst of Jordan, in the place where the feet of the priests which bare the ark of the covenant stood: and they are there unto this day. 10 For the priests which bare the ark stood in the midst of Jordan, until everything was finished that the Lord commanded Joshua to speak unto the people, according to all that Moses commanded Joshua: and the people hasted and passed over. 11 And it came to pass, when all the people were clean passed over, that the ark of the Lord passed over, and the priests, in the presence of the people.

4.8-11 The ark. The force of nature bowed in deference to the Ark, which represented the power of God. What man can turn the force of a river at overflow stage? This was a display of supernatural power. When the ark and it's power encountered the river and it's power, the ark turned away the river. This message was powerful. If the presence of God can turn a river at full tide, it can lead us to any victory. If the people had not been obedient, the supernatural power of the presence of God would have been wasted. Their part was to gather the stones and build a memorial. Their obedience was the catalyst that ignited the power of God. The great power of atomic weapons are ignited by a small fire. It is required to utilize the incredible power of the atomic weapon. Without a starter, the bomb is powerless. The power of God here at the overflowing banks, is ignited by the obedience of the people. It is ever so. Our obedience is the fire that starts the power of God operating in our lives. The power is in the details. The priests followed their instructions to the letter and God responded with an incredible display of supernatural power. The stone memorial was to remind them of this great miracle of the water crossing, but it also reminded them of the necessity of observing the smallest nuance of obedience. The power is packaged in obedience.

4.12-24 And the children of Reuben, and the children of Gad, and half the tribe of Manasseh, passed over armed before the children of Israel, as Moses spake unto them: 13 About forty thousand prepared for war passed over before the Lord unto battle, to the plains of Jericho. 14 On that day the Lord magnified Joshua in the sight of all Israel; and they feared him, as they feared Moses, all the days of his life. 15 And the Lord spake unto Joshua, saying, 16 Command the priests that bear the ark of the testimony, that they come up out of Jordan. 17 Joshua therefore commanded the priests, saying, Come ye up out of Jordan. 18 And it came to pass, when the priests that bare the ark of the covenant of the Lord were come

up out of the midst of Jordan, and the soles of the priests' feet were lifted up unto the dry land, that the waters of Jordan returned unto their place, and flowed over all his banks, as they did before. 19 And the people came up out of Jordan on the tenth day of the first month, and encamped in Gilgal, in the east border of Jericho. 20 And those twelve stones, which they took out of Jordan, did Joshua pitch in Gilgal. 21 And he spake unto the children of Israel, saying, When your children shall ask their fathers in time to come, saying, What mean these stones? 22 Then ye shall let your children know, saying, Israel came over this Jordan on dry land. 23 For the Lord your God dried up the waters of Jordan from before you, until ye were passed over, as the Lord your God did to the Red sea, which he dried up from before us, until we were gone over: 24 That all the people of the earth might know the hand of the Lord, that it is mighty: that ye might fear the Lord your God for ever.

4.12-24 Joshua. The voice of God through his chosen leader. The river is standing like a wall of water. Joshua commands the priests to come out on the land. When they set foot on the bank of the river, Joshua commands the water to flow as usual. The people saw with their own eyes that at the voice command of Joshua, the river acquiesced and obeyed. As long as this generation lived this moment would be imprinted on their minds. The Bible records that as long as this generation lived they followed the Lord. (Jud 2.7). As the ark came up onto the bank of the Promised Land, the river resumed. They had crossed over. They were committed. God had assured them He was their guide and provider. They carried the stones the five miles to Gilgal and built their memorial. Some modern archaeologists believe this is etiological myth. The Bible records they took the stones and built the memorial at

Gilgal. Gilgal was in the plains of Jericho on the east side. Abraham built his first altar at Gilgal. Saul was confirmed king at Gilgal. Here the Israelites kept the first Passover in the land and circumcised those born in the desert. This circumcision rolled away the reproach of Egyptian slavery. It is at Gilgal the Tabernacle is set up until it was moved to Shiloh. Joshua proclaims the memorial to be a reminder to their children of the power of God. Gilgal became a place of the school of the prophets (2 K 4.38). Six to seven hundred years later the prophets speak of people who made this memorial a source of idolatry (Hos 4.15, 9.15). It is a sad epithet that Gilgal with such a storied history eventually becomes a placed hated by God (Hos 9.15).

Chapter 5

5.1-9 And it came to pass, when all the kings of the Amorites, which were on the side of Jordan westward, and all the kings of the Canaanites, which were by the sea, heard that the Lord had dried up the waters of Jordan from before the children of Israel, until we were passed over, that their heart melted, neither was there spirit in them any more, because of the children of Israel. 2 At that time the Lord said unto Joshua, Make thee sharp knives, and circumcise again the children of Israel the second time. 3 And Joshua made him sharp knives, and circumcised the children of Israel at the hill of the foreskins. 4 And this is the cause why Joshua did circumcise: All the people that came out of Egypt, that were males, even all the men of war, died in the wilderness by the way, after they came out of Egypt. 5 Now all the people that came out were circumcised: but all the people that were born in the wilderness by the way as they came forth out of Egypt, them they had not circumcised. 6 For the children of Israel walked forty years in the wilderness, till all the people that were men of war, which came out of Egypt, were consumed, because they obeyed not the voice of the Lord: unto whom the Lord sware that he would not shew them the land, which the Lord sware unto their fathers that he would give us, a land that floweth with milk and honey. 7 And their children, whom he raised up in their stead, them Joshua circumcised: for they were uncircumcised, because they had not circumcised them by the way. 8 And it came to pass, when they had done circumcising all the people, that they abode in their places in the camp, till they were whole. 9 And the Lord said unto Joshua, This day have I rolled away the reproach of Egypt from off you. Wherefore the name of the place is called Gilgal unto this day.

5.1-9 Circumcision. When the people crossed into the land there was a need to renew the covenant. This had not been done for 40 years. Crossing the river had been a renewal and a new beginning. Circumcision was the sign of the covenant given to Abraham. In the New Testament, baptism is circumcision (Col 2.11-12), and is the sign of the covenant given unto the children of Abraham, the church (Gal 3.6-7). God informed the Israelites he had rolled away their reproach (scorn, taunt) from Egypt. The place is called Gilgal, which means the rolling away.

5.10-12 And the children of Israel encamped in Gilgal, and kept the passover on the fourteenth day of the month at even in the plains of Jericho. 11 And they did eat of the old corn of the land on the morrow after the passover, unleavened cakes, and parched corn in the selfsame day. 12 And the manna ceased on the morrow after they had eaten of the old corn of the land; neither had the children of Israel manna any more; but they did eat of the fruit of the land of Canaan that year.

5.10-12 The Passover and the manna. These two elements are here grouped together in the text. Old corn was eaten because new corn had not been sanctified unto the Lord as per the law. Lev 23.11 required the priest to wave the sheaf before the Lord first, before the corn was eaten. This could not be done until after the Sabbath so they could not use new corn, as it had not been sanctified. The cessation of manna, which represents the flesh of Jesus Christ, is an important moment. Jesus declared in John 6.58 that he was the manna sent from heaven. Jesus went back to heaven after His resurrection (Acts 1.9). With the coming of the Holy Ghost (which is the spirit of the departed one, Jesus Christ), believers cross over into the spiritual land of promise, and the manna (literal presence of Jesus) had to cease. The Apostle Paul informs the church that all these things happened unto them for ensamples (1Cor 10.11), which is a model of the true that was to come. Therefore, after the Passover lamb, which is Jesus (Jn 1.29), was offered on Calvary, it was necessary the manna cease. The coming plan of God, a millennium and a half in the future, was here being graphically enacted as an ensample for the church to understand God's master plan.

5.13-15 And it came to pass, when Joshua was by Jericho, that he lifted up his eyes and looked, and, behold, there stood a man over against him with his sword drawn in his hand: and Joshua went unto him, and said unto him, Art thou for us, or for our adversaries? 14 And he said, Nay; but as captain of the host of the Lord am I now come. And Joshua fell on his face to the earth, and did worship, and said unto him, What saith my Lord unto his servant? 15 And the captain of the Lord's host said unto Joshua, Loose thy shoe from off thy foot; for the place whereon thou standest is holy. And Joshua did so.

5.13-15 The captain of the host. This brief interlude is of great interest. It is documented but also not explained who this is. It certainly sets forth that God is with them and confirms His presence by the visible appearance of the captain of the host of the Lord. Who this captain is, is the subject of conjecture. One possibility is that it is a theophany, a temporary manifestation of God because Joshua is told to remove his shoe for he is on holy ground. This is a reference to when Moses encountered the burning bush. Jesus Christ is called the captain of our salvation in Heb 2.10. Jesus Christ also rides a white horse and leads the armies of heaven when he returns in Rev 19.11. This supports the idea of a theophany. Another possibility is Michael the archangel who is the warring angel of the Bible. There are only four angels named in the Bible even though there are an untold number of angels. Those named are Lucifer, Michael, Gabriel, and Apollyon. These angels are all assigned specific roles. Gabriel is the messenger angel and always brings messages (Dan 9.21, Lu 1.19). Lucifer was the angel of music and worship, who is now replaced by the church after his fall. Apollyon is the King of the bottomless pit in the book of Revelation (9.11). Michael is the warring angel. We see his role in fighting in the book of Daniel (10.13) and in the book of Jude (1.9). These defined roles in the scriptures place Michael the Archangel as a strong possibility. This event is not unique in the Old Testament. There are numerous times angels spoke and interacted with people. Examples would be Gideon, Samson's parents, Jacob, and even Balaam.

Chapter 6

6.1 Now Jericho was straitly shut up because of the children of Israel: none went out, and none came in.

6.1 Jericho. Jericho is one of the oldest cities in the world. It is on the plain in the Jordan Valley, at the base of the Judean mountains. It is approximately 8 miles northwest of the Dead Sea, and it is 800 feet below sea level. It only receives a few inches of rainfall a year. Yet, it is an oasis known as the city of palm trees. Jericho was the first city to be conquered in the new land. God plainly says that no spoil should be taken in Jericho; all the spoil of this city belongs to God. This reinforces the issue of first fruits. All of the spoil taken in the first city was to be given to God. Later this city would become a community of the prophets in the days of Elijah and Elisha.

6.2-5 And the Lord said unto Joshua, See, I have given into thine hand Jericho, and the king thereof, and the mighty men of valour. 3 And ye shall compass the city, all ye men of war, and go round about the city once. Thus shalt thou do six days. 4 And seven priests shall bear before the ark seven trumpets of rams' horns: and the seventh day ye shall compass the city seven times, and the priests shall blow with the trumpets. 5 And it shall

come to pass, that when they make a long blast with the ram's horn, and when ye hear the sound of the trumpet, all the people shall shout with a great shout; and the wall of the city shall fall down flat, and the people shall ascend up every man straight before him.

6.2-5 Instructions for war. God gave explicit instructions for the conquest of this city. The people were to march around in silence once a day for six days led by the priests who carried ram's horns. On the seventh day they were to march seven times, then sound the trumpets and give a great shout. This episode was to demonstrate to the Israelites that god is fighting their battles for them so there is no cause for fear.

6.6-10 And Joshua the son of Nun called the priests, and said unto them, Take up the ark of the covenant, and let seven priests bear seven trumpets of rams' horns before the ark of the Lord. 7 And he said unto the people, Pass on, and compass the city, and let him that is armed pass on before the ark of the Lord. 8 And it came to pass, when Joshua had spoken unto the people, that the seven priests bearing the seven trumpets of rams' horns passed on before the Lord, and blew with the trumpets: and the ark of the covenant of the Lord followed them. 9 And the armed men went before the priests that blew with the trumpets, and the rereward came after the ark, the priests going on, and blowing with the trumpets. 10 And Joshua had commanded the people, saying, Ye shall not shout, nor make any noise with your voice, neither shall any word proceed out of your mouth, until the day I bid you shout; then shall ye shout.

6.6-10 The march. It was quite a sight. Seven priests blowing rams horns, the armed men quietly marching, followed by the ark of the covenant, followed by the remainder of men. The men with no weapons were not excused from the march. Deut 20.1-4 had been spoken by Moses for just this sort of battle. The Lord was going before them.

6.11-27 So the ark of the Lord compassed the city, going about it once: and they came into the camp, and lodged in the camp. 12 And Joshua rose early in the morning, and the priests took up the ark of the Lord. 13 And seven priests bearing seven trumpets of rams' horns before the ark of the Lord went on continually, and blew with the trumpets: and the armed men went before them; but the rereward came after the ark of the Lord, the priests going on, and blowing with the trumpets. 14 And the second day they compassed the city once, and returned into the camp: so they did six days. 15 And it came to pass on the seventh day, that they rose early about the dawning of the day, and compassed the city after the same manner seven times: only on that day they compassed the city seven times. 16 And it came to pass at the seventh time, when the priests blew with the trumpets, Joshua said unto the people, Shout; for the Lord hath given you the city. 17 And the city shall be accursed, even it, and all that are therein, to the Lord: only Rahab the harlot shall live, she and all that are with her in the house, because she hid the messengers that we sent. 18 And ye, in any wise keep yourselves from the accursed thing, lest ye make yourselves accursed, when ye take of the accursed thing, and make the camp of Israel a curse, and trouble it. 19 But all the silver, and gold, and vessels of brass and iron, are consecrated unto the Lord: they shall come into the treasury of the Lord. 20 So the people shouted when the priests blew with the trumpets: and it came to pass, when the people heard the sound of the trumpet, and the people shouted with a great shout, that the wall fell

down flat, so that the people went up into the city, every man straight before him, and they took the city. 21 And they utterly destroyed all that was in the city, both man and woman, young and old, and ox, and sheep, and ass, with the edge of the sword. 22 But Joshua had said unto the two men that had spied out the country, Go into the harlot's house, and bring out thence the woman, and all that she hath, as ye sware unto her. 23 And the young men that were spies went in, and brought out Rahab, and her father, and her mother, and her brethren, and all that she had; and they brought out all her kindred, and left them without the camp of Israel. 24 And they burnt the city with fire, and all that was therein: only the silver, and the gold, and the vessels of brass and of iron, they put into the treasury of the house of the Lord. 25 And Joshua saved Rahab the harlot alive, and her father's household, and all that she had; and she dwelleth in Israel even unto this day; because she hid the messengers, which Joshua sent to spy out Jericho. 26 And Joshua adjured them at that time, saying, Cursed be the man before the Lord, that riseth up and buildeth this city Jericho: he shall lay the foundation thereof in his firstborn, and in his youngest son shall he set up the gates of it. 27 So the Lord was with Joshua; and his fame was noised throughout all the country.

6.11-27 The victory. The battle unfolded as announced and the victory was complete. Rahab and those she protected were spared and everything else is destroyed completely. This sent a message to the other cities of Palestine of the futility of resisting the army of Israel. God was fighting this war. There was no prolonged siege. There was no traditional warfare. The world had never seen this type of conquest. Jericho was the gateway to the land. When it collapsed via a miraculous intervention by God, it sent shock waves throughout the land. Why was the battle campaign seven days? God was about to create a new nation that would follow His laws and be His special people in the earth. He mirrored the original creation by following the same time template of seven days. As Adam flawed the original creation, so Achan would flaw this new creation.

Chapter 7

7.1 But the children of Israel committed a trespass in the accursed thing: for Achan, the son of Carmi, the son of Zabdi, the son of Zerah, of the tribe of Judah, took of the accursed thing: and the anger of the Lord was kindled against the children of Israel.

7.1. Achan. Achan is also known as Achar, which means the troubler of Israel. His sin was imputed to the whole nation because Israel was under dual responsibility. Israel was responsible for corporate obedience as well as individual responsibility. This sin was the cause of the defeat at Ai. God wanted Israel to know that one person did affect the entire nation.

7.2-9 And Joshua sent men from Jericho to Ai, which is beside Bethaven, on the east of Bethel, and spake unto them, saying, Go up and view the country. And the men went up and viewed Ai. 3 And they returned to Joshua, and said unto him, Let not all the people go up; but let about two or three thousand men go up and smite Ai; and make not all the people to labour thither; for they are but few. 4 So there went up thither of the people about three thousand men: and they fled before the men of Ai. 5 And the men of Ai smote of them about thirty and six men:

for they chased them from before the gate even unto Shebarim, and smote them in the going down: wherefore the hearts of the people melted, and became as water. 6 And Joshua rent his clothes, and fell to the earth upon his face before the ark of the Lord until the eventide, he and the elders of Israel, and put dust upon their heads. 7 And Joshua said, Alas, O Lord God, wherefore hast thou at all brought this people over Jordan, to deliver us into the hand of the Amorites, to destroy us? would to God we had been content, and dwelt on the other side Jordan! 8 O Lord, what shall I say, when Israel turneth their backs before their enemies! 9 For the Canaanites and all the inhabitants of the land shall hear of it, and shall environ us round, and cut off our name from the earth: and what wilt thou do unto thy great name?

7.2-9 Ai. The shock of this loss was immense. A small insignificant city defeated Israel on their second battle. Ai was where Abraham had first pitched his tent and built an altar (Gen 12.8, 13.3-4). God tells Joshua the cause of their defeat is sin in the camp.

7.10-26 And the Lord said unto Joshua, Get thee up; wherefore liest thou thus upon thy face? 11 Israel hath sinned, and they have also transgressed my covenant which I commanded them: for they have even taken of the accursed thing, and have also stolen, and dissembled also, and they have put it even among their own stuff. 12 Therefore the children of Israel could not stand before their enemies, but turned their backs before their enemies, because they were accursed: neither will I be with you any more, except ye destroy the accursed from among you. 13 Up, sanctify the people, and say, Sanctify yourselves against to morrow: for thus saith the Lord God of Israel, There is an accursed thing in the midst of thee, O Israel: thou canst not stand before thine enemies, until ye take away the accursed thing from among you. 14 In the morning therefore ye shall be brought according to your tribes: and it shall be, that the tribe which the Lord taketh shall come according to the families thereof; and the family which the Lord shall take shall come by households; and the household which the Lord shall take shall come man by man. 15 And it shall be, that he that is taken with the accursed thing shall be burnt with fire, he and all that he hath: because he hath transgressed the covenant of the Lord, and because he hath wrought folly in Israel. 16 So Joshua rose up early in the morning, and brought Israel by their tribes; and the tribe of Judah was taken: 17 And he brought the family of Judah; and he took the family of the Zarhites: and he brought the family of the Zarhites man by man; and Zabdi was taken: 18 And he brought his household man by man; and Achan, the son of Carmi, the son of Zabdi, the son of Zerah, of the tribe of Judah, was taken. 19 And Joshua said unto Achan, My son, give, I pray thee, glory to the Lord God of Israel, and make confession unto him; and tell me now what thou hast done; hide it not from me. 20 And Achan answered Joshua, and said, Indeed I have sinned against the Lord God of Israel, and thus and thus have I done: 21 When I saw among the spoils a goodly Babylonish garment, and two hundred shekels of silver, and a wedge of gold of fifty shekels weight, then I coveted them, and took them; and, behold, they are hid in the earth in the midst of my tent, and the silver under it. 22 So Joshua sent messengers, and they ran unto the tent; and, behold, it was hid in his tent, and the silver under it. 23 And they took them out of the midst of the tent, and brought them unto Joshua, and unto all the children of Israel, and laid them out before the Lord. 24 And Joshua, and all Israel with him, took Achan the son

of Zerah, and the silver, and the garment, and the wedge of gold, and his sons, and his daughters, and his oxen, and his asses, and his sheep, and his tent, and all that he had: and they brought them unto the valley of Achor. 25 And Joshua said, Why hast thou troubled us? the Lord shall trouble thee this day. And all Israel stoned him with stones, and burned them with fire, after they had stoned them with stones. 26 And they raised over him a great heap of stones unto this day. So the Lord turned from the fierceness of his anger. Wherefore the name of that place was called, The valley of Achor, unto this day.

7.10-26 The casting of the lot. Joshua and the people were deeply affected. There was first of all the loss of thirty-six men, but more importantly Israel had lost their invincible shield. They had been beaten, so the obvious conclusion was that God had withdrawn His help, for God cannot be defeated. Joshua prays for understanding while making mild complaints. God replies Israel must purge the camp of the sin. The guilty person must be discovered, stoned and burned. The method used to ferret out the offender was casting lots. It began with tribes, then moved to families, and finally to the guilty man. The Lot fell upon Achan. When challenged, Achan confesses. The purloined items are uncovered and brought as evidence. Achan and all his family and possessions, are stoned and burned. The method of how the lot worked is not clear. One possibility was small tablets were used like ballots and drawn out. This seems to be how other lots worked (18.11, 19.1). In the charge of war given by Joshua (6.18), the pilfered objects were called accursed. The principal here was when they took a sacred item that was set-aside to God and claimed ownership, it brought a curse on them. It was stealing at the highest possible level. To steal from God made the thief accursed (dedicated to destruction). Achan not only lost what he had stolen, but also lost everything else. Thus is the result of all who steal from God. Deut 13.16-17 gives the law of the ban concerning a cursed town. This was applied to this family unit. The shadow of the curse engulfed everything claimed by Achan. The anger of the Lord was assuaged. The mound of stones is named the valley of Achor.

Chapter 8

8.1-9 And the Lord said unto Joshua, Fear not, neither be thou dismayed: take all the people of war with thee, and arise, go up to Ai: see, I have given into thy hand the king of Ai, and his people, and his city, and his land: 2 And thou shalt do to Ai and her king as thou didst unto Jericho and her king: only the spoil thereof, and the cattle thereof, shall ye take for a prey unto yourselves: lay thee an ambush for the city behind it. 3 So Joshua arose, and all the people of war, to go up against Ai: and Joshua chose out thirty thousand mighty men of valour, and sent them away by night. 4 And he commanded them, saying, Behold, ye shall lie in wait against the city, even behind the city: go not very far from the city, but be ye all ready: 5 And I, and all the people that are with me, will approach unto the city: and it shall come to pass, when they come out against us, as at the first, that we will flee before them, 6 (For they will come out after us) till we have drawn them from the city; for they will say, They flee before us, as at the first: therefore we will flee before them. 7 Then ye shall rise up from the ambush, and seize upon the city: for the Lord your God will deliver it into your hand. 8 And it shall be, when ye have taken the city, that ye shall set the city on fire: according to the commandment of the Lord shall ye do. See, I have commanded you. 9 Joshua therefore sent them forth: and they went to lie in ambush, and abode between Bethel and Ai, on the west side of Ai: but Joshua lodged that night among the people.

8.1-9 The ambush. God instructs Joshua to go and take Ai. God does not give the plan of battle for Ai because it is not his. He has given it to the people. Joshua takes charge and plans the battle. It is an ambush with Israel appearing to be routed again, but this time it is a ruse, and Ai falls into the trap.

8.10-29 And Joshua rose up early in the morning, and numbered the people, and went up, he and the elders of Israel, before the people to Ai. 11 And all the people, even the people of war that were with him, went up, and drew nigh, and came before the city, and pitched on the north side of Ai: now there was a valley between them and Ai. 12 And he took about five thousand men, and set them to lie in ambush between Bethel and Ai, on the west side of the city. 13 And when they had set the people, even all the host that was on the north of the city, and their liers in wait on the west of the city, Joshua went that night into the midst of the valley. 14 And it came to pass, when the king of Ai saw it, that they hasted and rose up early, and the men of the city went out against Israel to battle, he and all his people, at a time appointed, before the plain; but he wist not that there were liers in ambush against him behind the city. 15 And Joshua and all Israel made as if they were beaten before them, and fled by the way of the wilderness. 16 And all the people that were in Ai were called together to pursue after them: and they pursued after Joshua, and were drawn away from the city. 17 And there was not a man left in Ai or Bethel, that went not out after Israel: and they left the city open, and pursued after Israel. 18 And the Lord said unto Joshua, Stretch out the spear that is in thy hand toward Ai; for I will give it into thine hand. And Joshua stretched out the spear that he had in his hand toward the city. 19 And the ambush arose quickly out of their place, and they ran as soon as he had stretched out his hand: and they entered into the city, and took it, and hasted and set the city on fire. 20 And when the men of Ai looked behind them, they saw, and, behold, the smoke of the city ascended up to heaven, and they had no power to flee this way or that way: and the people that fled to the wilderness turned back upon the pursuers. 21 And when Joshua and all Israel saw that the ambush had taken the city, and that the smoke of the city ascended, then they turned again, and slew the men of Ai. 22 And the other issued out of the city against them; so they were in the midst of Israel, some on this side, and some on that side: and they smote them, so that they let none of them remain or escape. 23 And the king of Ai they took alive, and brought him to Joshua. 24 And it came to pass, when Israel had made an end of slaying all the inhabitants of Ai in the field, in the wilderness wherein they chased them, and when they were all fallen on the edge of the sword, until they were consumed, that all the Israelites returned unto Ai, and smote it with the edge of the sword. 25 And so it was, that all that fell that day, both of men and women, were twelve thousand, even all the men of Ai. 26 For Joshua drew not his hand back, wherewith he stretched out the spear, until he had utterly destroyed all the inhabitants of Ai. 27 Only the cattle and the spoil of that city Israel took for a prey unto themselves, according unto the word of the Lord which he commanded Joshua. 28 And Joshua burnt Ai, and made it an heap for ever, even a desolation unto this day. 29 And the king of Ai he hanged on a tree until eventide: and as soon as the sun was down, Joshua commanded that they should take his carcase down from the tree, and cast it at the entering of the gate of the city, and raise thereon a great heap of stones, that remaineth unto this day.

8.10-29 The battle. The ruse worked and Ai was lured into the trap set by Israel. Once the inhabitants of Ai and Bethel were out of the city in pursuit of Israel, the men in ambush entered the city and set it on fire. When Joshua saw the smoke he stretched forth his spear and held it up until the entire population of men of these cities were killed. The king of Ai was captured, hanged, and left there until sundown. The people were allowed to keep the spoil of war. The sad epitaph of this engagement was everything Achan wanted he could have had if he had waited on the time God put His blessing on it. In some ways this victory over Ai with only twelve thousand men was sweeter than the victory over Jericho because it re-established that God was again fighting for Israel. This leads to Joshua renewing the covenant with the Lord.

8.30-35 Then Joshua built an altar unto the Lord God of Israel in mount Ebal, 31 As Moses the servant of the Lord commanded the children of Israel, as it is written in the book of the law of Moses, an altar of whole stones, over which no man hath lift up any iron: and they offered thereon burnt offerings unto the Lord, and sacrificed peace offerings. 32 And he wrote there upon the stones a copy of the law of Moses, which he wrote in the presence of the children of Israel. 33 And all Israel, and their elders, and officers, and their judges, stood on this side the ark and on that side before the priests the Levites, which bare the ark of the covenant of the Lord,

as well the stranger, as he that was born among them; half of them over against mount Gerizim, and half of them over against mount Ebal; as Moses the servant of the Lord had commanded before, that they should bless the people of Israel. 34 And afterward he read all the words of the law, the blessings and cursings, according to all that is written in the book of the law. 35 There was not a word of all that Moses commanded, which Joshua read not before all the congregation of Israel, with the women, and the little ones, and the strangers that were conversant among them.

8.30-35 Renewing the covenant. Joshua builds an altar of whole stones that have not been molded by man. There the people offer burnt offerings and sacrificed peace offerings. Joshua made some pillars and on these pillars he wrote the blessings and curses of the Decalogue. The war was halted for a while so the people could recommit to their complete obedience. In Deut 27.2-4 Moses had instructed Joshua to build an altar after crossing the Jordan and to set up the covenant, and to write the law and cover it with plaister. The suspension of war is a given because of the distance the people had to journey to Ebal and then return to Gilgal. This episode is important for it forever connected the altar and the law together. Many years later Jesus would reinforce this combination in the New Testament era. Jesus proclaimed people must worship God in spirit and in truth (Jn 4.24). The altar represented the spirit, and the law represented the truth. The valley where this occurred is a beautiful place and the two mountains provide a natural amphitheater that can accommodate a large group of people. The sides of the mountains are step like, and provide natural seating. When seated or standing on one mountain and speaking antiphonally, the people on the other mountain can hear clearly. The entire contingent of the nation was gathered together and affirmed their allegiance to God and His Law. It was now time to continue the war of liberation.

Chapter 9

9.1-15 And it came to pass, when all the kings which were on this side Jordan, in the hills, and in the valleys, and in all the coasts of the great sea over against Lebanon, the Hittite, and the Amorite, the Canaanite, the Perizzite, the Hivite, and the Jebusite, heard thereof; 2 That they gathered themselves together, to fight with Joshua and with Israel, with one accord. 3 And when the inhabitants of Gibeon heard what Joshua had done unto Jericho and to Ai, 4 They did work wilily, and went and made as if they had been ambassadors, and took old sacks upon their asses, and wine bottles, old, and rent, and bound up; 5 And old shoes and clouted upon their feet, and old garments upon them; and all the bread of their provision was dry and mouldy. 6 And they went to Joshua unto the camp at Gilgal, and said unto him, and to the men of Israel, We be come from a far country: now therefore make ye a league with us. 7 And the men of Israel said unto the Hivites, Peradventure ye dwell among us; and how shall we make a league with you? 8 And they said unto Joshua, We are thy servants. And Joshua said unto them, Who are ye? and from whence come ye? 9 And they said unto him, From a very far country thy servants are come because of the name of the Lord thy God: for we have heard the fame of him, and all that he did in Egypt,

10 And all that he did to the two kings of the Amorites, that were beyond Jordan, to Sihon king of Heshbon, and to Og king of Bashan, which was at Ashtaroth. 11 Wherefore our elders and all the inhabitants of our country spake to us, saying, Take victuals with you for the journey, and go to meet them, and say unto them, We are your servants: therefore now make ye a league with us. 12 This our bread we took hot for our provision out of our houses on the day we came forth to go unto you; but now, behold, it is dry, and it is mouldy: 13 And these bottles of wine, which we filled, were new; and, behold, they be rent: and these our garments and our shoes are become old by reason of the very long journey. 14 And the men took of their victuals, and asked not counsel at the mouth of the Lord. 15 And Joshua made peace with them, and made a league with them, to let them live: and the princes of the congregation sware unto them.

9.1-15 Gibeonites. This deception is put here in the narrative either by sequence of time or to illustrate the futility of not seeking the counsel of God. It shares the same ideology of Ai in that when the leaders did not ask council of God they followed wrong paths. Both times there were consequences. The Gibeonites were prepared and produced evidence to support their bogus claim for a peace treaty. When the people of Israel learned of this situation, there was murmuring against the princes. No one had forgot the humiliation of Ai, and here they were again facing a similar result and the people feared the backlash of an angry God. This was an important moment for the fledging nation. It made them realize there are more kinds of warfare than swords and shields. It revealed Israel was not ready for this kind of warfare. The spiritual analogy is that many things are accepted into the church by presenting themselves as helpful and harmless. Modern technology must be carefully looked at for it comes in this manner. When things like TV and the internet bring the environment that is displeasing to God, and contrary to his promises, this technology must not be compromised with.

9.16-27 And it came to pass at the end of three days after they had made a league with them, that they heard that they were their neighbours, and that they dwelt among them. 17 And the children of Israel journeyed, and came unto their cities on the third day. Now their cities were Gibeon, and Chephirah, and Beeroth, and Kirjathjearim. 18 And the children of Israel smote them not, because the princes of the congregation had sworn unto them by the Lord God of Israel. And all the congregation murmured against the princes. 19 But all the princes said unto all the congregation, We have sworn unto them by the Lord God of Israel: now therefore we may not touch them. 20 This we will do to them; we will even let them live, lest wrath be upon us, because of the oath which we sware unto them. 21 And the princes said unto them, Let them live; but let them be hewers of wood and drawers of water unto all the congregation; as the princes had promised them. 22 And Joshua called for them, and he spake unto them, saying, Wherefore have ye beguiled us, saying, We are very far from you; when ye dwell among us? 23 Now therefore ye are cursed, and there shall none of you be freed from being bondmen, and hewers of wood and drawers of water for the house of my God. 24 And they answered Joshua, and said, Because it was certainly told thy servants, how that the Lord thy God commanded his servant Moses to give you all the land, and to destroy all the inhabitants of the land from before you, therefore we were sore afraid of our lives because of you, and have done this thing. 25 And now, behold, we are in thine

hand: as it seemeth good and right unto thee to do unto us, do. 26 And so did he unto them, and delivered them out of the hand of the children of Israel, that they slew them not. 27 And Joshua made them that day hewers of wood and drawers of water for the congregation, and for the altar of the Lord, even unto this day, in the place which he should choose.

9.16-27 The compromise. This is a universal temptation. It is always a temptation to make the things we compromise with our servants, and make our life tasks easier. Humanly we find a way to allow it and call it harmless. We feel we can control it. Here the leaders found themselves in a conundrum. On one hand they were to annihilate the nations of the land because of their gods and their sinful influence. On the other hand they had foolishly given their word as a pledge. They were caught without a solution to escape the quagmire. They sought a way out of the imbroglio. It is difficult to grasp why the leaders felt this way. The agreement with the Gibeonites was founded upon a lie. The Gibeonites had boldly lied. The children of Israel were forbidden to make treaties with the people of the land. It would seem easy to just deny their appeal and destroy these liars and charlatans. The reticence on the part of Israel appears to be that they had given their pledge unto the Gibeonites by the Lord God of Israel. In the larger picture, they would have brought the name of the Lord God of Israel into contempt in the eyes of the Canaanites. They had sworn by God and His sincerity was the issue. Their impudent actions of taking their victuals led them into a hasty, regrettable decision. The food of the forbidden always appeals to the flesh. Now they were faced with an unreconcilable dilemma. To break their vow would also be a sin. The old adage two wrongs do not make a right applies here. So Israel compromised. In their defense, there is much to be said about keeping an oath (Ps 15.4). Historically there does not appear any recorded writings that show this decision ever came back to haunt Israel. These Gibeonites placed in the service of God, are never recorded to induce Israel to idolatry. In fact, later when Saul attempts to destroy them, God himself defends this people (2 Sam 21.1). Israel was learning there are many kinds of war.

Chapter 10

10.1-5 Now it came to pass, when Adonizedec king of Jerusalem had heard how Joshua had taken Ai, and had utterly destroyed it; as he had done to Jericho and her king, so he had done to Ai and her king; and how the inhabitants of Gibeon had made peace with Israel, and were among them; 2 That they feared greatly, because Gibeon was a great city, as one of the royal cities, and because it was greater than Ai, and all the men thereof were mighty. 3 Wherefore Adonizedec king of Jerusalem, sent unto Hoham king of Hebron, and unto Piram king of Jarmuth, and unto Japhia king of Lachish, and unto Debir king of Eglon, saying, 4 Come up unto me, and help me, that we may smite Gibeon: for it hath made peace with Joshua and with the children of Israel. 5 Therefore the five kings of the Amorites, the king of Jerusalem, the king of Hebron, the king of Jarmuth, the king of Lachish, the king of Eglon, gathered themselves together, and went up, they and all their hosts, and encamped before Gibeon, and made war against it.

10.1-5 Attack upon Gibeon. The ripples of fear are widening through out the land of Ammon. These Ammonite kings have carefully watched the unfolding drama invading their land, and decide it is time to take it serious. They form a league and decide to attack Gibeon. This will slow the invasion of Israel. Adonizedek, king of Jerusalem is a descendant of Melchizedek. His name is a form of Melchizedek and both mean king of righteousness. This king's ancestor is the one who met Abraham after the battle in Gen. 14, and to whom Abraham paid tithes. Time had eroded their feelings of loyalty to Abraham and his line. Abraham's burial site was on their land at a place called Khalil, which means friend of God. This was a reference to Abraham's sojourn there. The inhabitants of Jerusalem were known as Jebusites. This people would possess the city of Jerusalem until the reign of king David. The federation of these kings was comprised of the southern part of the land from Jerusalem southward.

10.6-15 And the men of Gibeon sent unto Joshua to the camp to Gilgal, saying, Slack not thy hand from thy servants; come up to us quickly, and save us, and help us: for all the kings of the Amorites that dwell in the mountains are gathered together against us. 7 So Joshua ascended from Gilgal, he, and all the people of war with him, and all the mighty men of valour. 8 And the Lord said unto Joshua, Fear them not: for I have delivered them into thine hand; there shall not a man of them stand before thee. 9 Joshua therefore came unto them suddenly, and went up from Gilgal all night. 10 And the Lord discomfited them before Israel, and slew them with a great slaughter at Gibeon, and chased them along the way that goeth up to Bethhoron, and smote them to Azekah, and unto Makkedah. 11 And it came to pass, as they fled from before Israel, and were in the going down to Bethhoron, that the Lord cast down great stones from heaven upon them unto Azekah, and they died: they were more which died with hailstones than they whom the children of Israel slew with the sword. 12

Then spake Joshua to the Lord in the day when the Lord delivered up the Amorites before the children of Israel, and he said in the sight of Israel, Sun, stand thou still upon Gibeon; and thou, Moon, in the valley of Ajalon. 13 And the sun stood still, and the moon stayed, until the people had avenged themselves upon their enemies. Is not this written in the book of Jasher? So the sun stood still in the midst of heaven, and hasted not to go down about a whole day. 14 And there was no day like that before it or after it, that the Lord hearkened unto the voice of a man: for the Lord fought for Israel. 15 And Joshua returned, and all Israel with him, unto the camp to Gilgal.

10.6-15 The sun stands still. The ensuing battle has an amazing event that takes place. Joshua prays that the sun not go down until he was able to take vengeance upon the Amorites. This in fact occurred. Joshua celebrates this event in a war song. The verses 12-15 are a quotation from the book of Jashur mentioned in verse 13. This book was a part of the Book of the wars of the Lord mentioned in Num 21.14. Here the strophes of a song are woven into the historical narrative. The book of Jashur is also mentioned in 2 Sam 1.18. This battle was also momentous because of the stones God cast down and killed many of the fleeing enemy. The largest hailstones on record weighed two pounds. In a storm in Bangladesh 92 people died from being hit with these hailstones in 1986. This confirms the Biblical account here in this chapter is not a fairy tale. God had again joined in the battle on the side of Israel. Verse 14 declares there was no day like it before or after when the Lord hearkened unto the voice of a man.

16.16-28 But these five kings fled, and hid themselves in a cave at Makkedah. 17 And it was told Joshua, saying,

The five kings are found hid in a cave at Makkedah. 18 And Joshua said, Roll great stones upon the mouth of the cave, and set men by it for to keep them: 19 And stay ye not, but pursue after your enemies, and smite the hindmost of them; suffer them not to enter into their cities: for the Lord your God hath delivered them into your hand. 20 And it came to pass, when Joshua and the children of Israel had made an end of slaying them with a very great slaughter, till they were consumed, that the rest which remained of them entered into fenced cities. 21 And all the people returned to the camp to Joshua at Makkedah in peace: none moved his tongue against any of the children of Israel. 22 Then said Joshua, Open the mouth of the cave, and bring out those five kings unto me out of the cave. 23 And they did so, and brought forth those five kings unto him out of the cave, the king of Jerusalem, the king of Hebron, the king of Jarmuth, the king of Lachish, and the king of Eglon. 24 And it came to pass, when they brought out those kings unto Joshua, that Joshua called for all the men of Israel, and said unto the captains of the men of war which went with him, Come near, put your feet upon the necks of these kings. And they came near, and put their feet upon the necks of them. 25 And Joshua said unto them, Fear not, nor be dismayed, be strong and of good courage: for thus shall the Lord do to all your enemies against whom ye fight. 26 And afterward Joshua smote them, and slew them, and hanged them on five trees: and they were hanging upon the trees until the evening. 27 And it came to pass at the time of the going down of the sun, that Joshua commanded, and they took them down off the trees, and cast them into the cave wherein they had been hid, and laid great stones in the cave's mouth, which remain until this very day. 28 And that day Joshua took Makkedah, and smote it with the edge of the sword, and the king thereof he utterly destroyed, them, and all the souls that were therein; he let none remain: and he did to the king of Makkedah as he did unto the king of Jericho.

10.16-28 Five kings. Somehow these five kings escaped the hailstones and the sword and hid themselves in a cave that was to become their mausoleum. Possibly they entered the cave before the hailstorm began. These kings discovered you can hide from Joshua and the army of Israel, but you cannot hide from God. Divine vengeance has an all seeing eye. Joshua has his leaders put their feet on the king's necks to show these, and all enemies, are subject to Israel. It is futile to flee for refuge from God. Joshua was unrelenting in his degradation of these kings. He was sending a message throughout the land of what was to come. On a spiritual note we are all at war daily with our flesh. The five kings we face are sight, sound, touch, smell, and taste. These five kings want to hide in a cave and be free but for our spiritual man to conquer, these kings of our flesh must be brought under subjection. There are other kings for us to overcome just like Joshua faced more kings. We will face King Anger, King Pride, King Falsehood, King Disobedience, and King Self. Our war of conquest is ongoing.

10.29-43 Then Joshua passed from Makkedah, and all Israel with him, unto Libnah, and fought against Libnah: 30 And the Lord delivered it also, and the king thereof, into the hand of Israel; and he smote it with the edge of the sword, and all the souls that were therein; he let none remain in it; but did unto the king thereof as he did unto the king of Jericho. 31 And Joshua passed from Libnah, and all Israel with him, unto Lachish, and encamped against it, and fought against it: 32 And the Lord delivered Lachish into the hand of Israel,

which took it on the second day, and smote it with the edge of the sword, and all the souls that were therein, according to all that he had done to Libnah. 33 Then Horam king of Gezer came up to help Lachish; and Joshua smote him and his people, until he had left him none remaining. 34 And from Lachish Joshua passed unto Eglon, and all Israel with him; and they encamped against it, and fought against it: 35 And they took it on that day, and smote it with the edge of the sword, and all the souls that were therein he utterly destroyed that day, according to all that he had done to Lachish. 36 And Joshua went up from Eglon, and all Israel with him, unto Hebron; and they fought against it: 37 And they took it, and smote it with the edge of the sword, and the king thereof, and all the cities thereof, and all the souls that were therein; he left none remaining, according to all that he had done to Eglon; but destroyed it utterly, and all the souls that were therein. 38 And Joshua returned, and all Israel with him, to Debir; and fought against it: 39 And he took it, and the king thereof, and all the cities thereof; and they smote them with the edge of the sword, and utterly destroyed all the souls that were therein; he left none remaining: as he had done to Hebron, so he did to Debir, and to the king thereof; as he had done also to Libnah, and to her king. 40 So Joshua smote all the country of the hills, and of the south, and of the vale, and of the springs, and all their kings: he left none remaining, but utterly destroyed all that breathed, as the Lord God of Israel commanded. 41 And Joshua smote them from Kadeshbarnea even unto Gaza, and all the country of Goshen, even unto Gibeon. 42 And all these kings and their land did Joshua take at one time, because the Lord God of Israel fought for Israel. 43 And Joshua returned, and all Israel with him, unto the camp to Gilgal.

10.29-43 Southern Canaan. When Israel crossed into the land they set up camp at Gilgal. From this base they made several major thrusts of war. They made one to the south, one to the north and one due west. These verses describe the thrust to the south. It began at Makkedah, then on to Libnah, then to Lachish, then to Eglon, then to Hebron, then to Debir. Joshua used a scorched earth policy and left none alive. Joshua and the armies of God took from Kadesh-barnea unto Gaza (this is from the south to the north on the western border), and all the country of Goshen unto Gibeon (south to north on the east side). So Joshua took the whole of the south of Canaan. He took all the districts, the mountains, the lowlands, the slopes, and the hills. The army then returned to Gilgal. This was one continual southern war thrust that lasted a long time (11.18).

Chapter 11

11.1-12 And it came to pass, when Jabin king of Hazor had heard those things, that he sent to Jobab king of Madon, and to the king of Shimron, and to the king of Achshaph, 2 And to the kings that were on the north of the mountains, and of the plains south of Chinneroth, and in the valley, and in the borders of Dor on the west, 3 And to the Canaanite on the east and on the west, and to the Amorite, and the Hittite, and the Perizzite, and the Jebusite in the mountains, and to the Hivite under Hermon in the land of Mizpeh. 4 And they went out, they and all their hosts with them, much people, even as the sand that is upon the sea shore in multitude, with horses and chariots very many. 5 And when all these kings were met together, they came and pitched together at the waters of Merom, to fight against Israel. 6 And the Lord said unto Joshua, Be not afraid because of them: for to morrow about this time will I deliver them up all slain before Israel: thou shalt hough their horses, and burn their chariots with fire. 7 So Joshua came, and all the people of war with him, against them by the waters of Merom suddenly; and they fell upon them. 8 And the Lord delivered them into the hand of Israel, who smote them, and chased them unto great Zidon, and unto Misrephothmaim, and unto the valley of Mizpeh eastward; and they smote them, until they left them none remaining. 9 And Joshua did unto them as the Lord bade him: he houghed their horses, and burnt their chariots with fire. 10 And Joshua at that time turned back, and took Hazor, and smote the king thereof with the sword: for Hazor beforetime was the head of all those kingdoms. 11 And they smote all the souls that were therein with the edge of the sword, utterly destroying them: there was not any left to breathe: and he burnt Hazor with fire. 12 And all the cities of those kings, and all the kings of them, did Joshua take, and smote them with the edge of the sword, and he utterly destroyed them, as Moses the servant of the Lord commanded.

11.1-12 The Northern campaign. This chapter relates how the army now turns north and subdues the rest of the land. God encouraged Joshua to fight them. God delivers them into the hand of Joshua and the inhabitants of the land are smitten. The king of Hazor organizes an alliance of kings to fight Joshua. Hazor was the head of these kingdoms (10). Later Hazor was restored (Jud 4.2, 1 Sam 12.9). This city was fortified by Solomon (1 K 9.15) and later conquered by Tiglath-Pileser (2 K 15.29). Josephus numbers the army against Joshua at 300,000 soldiers and 10,000 chariots. God had promised in Deut 32.30 that one should chase a thousand and two should put ten thousand to flight. This great battle joined at the waters of Merom. If Joshua had not made the decisions he did concerning Gibeon, this Northern coalition of foes possibly would have been much more formidable. By accepting the Gibeonites and sparing them, and protecting them against the attack by Adonizedek, Joshua effectively divided the country in half and conquered the country in two great thrusts. Had Joshua not done this, it is probable the kings of the south would have made alliance with the kings of the north and presented a foe of much greater challenge. If the entire country would have united as one alliance, the war could have taken a different path. God did for Joshua what he does for all. God in His compassion does not make anyone face all of life's problems at once. God partitions our battles so we can manage them piece meal. In this scenario, if Joshua's army had been attacked from the rear by the northern coalition while he fought the southern campaign, it would have provided a much more difficult war.

11.13-23 But as for the cities that stood still in their strength, Israel burned none of them, save Hazor only; that did Joshua burn. 14 And all the spoil of these cities, and the cattle, the children of Israel took for a prey unto themselves; but every man they smote with the edge of the sword, until they had destroyed them, neither left they any to breathe. 15 As the Lord commanded Moses his servant, so did Moses command Joshua, and so did Joshua; he left nothing undone of all that the Lord commanded Moses. 16 So Joshua took all that land, the hills, and all the south country, and all the land of Goshen, and the valley, and the plain, and the mountain of Israel, and the valley of the same; 17 Even from the mount Halak, that goeth up to Seir, even unto Baalgad in the valley of Lebanon under mount Hermon: and all their kings he took, and smote them, and slew them. 18 Joshua made war a long time with all those kings. 19 There was not a city that made peace with the children of Israel, save the Hivites the inhabitants of Gibeon: all other they took in battle. 20 For it was of the Lord to harden their hearts, that they should come against Israel in battle, that he might destroy them utterly, and that they might have no favour, but that he might destroy them, as the Lord commanded Moses. 21 And

at that time came Joshua, and cut off the Anakims from the mountains, from Hebron, from Debir, from Anab, and from all the mountains of Judah, and from all the mountains of Israel: Joshua destroyed them utterly with their cities. 22 There was none of the Anakims left in the land of the children of Israel: only in Gaza, in Gath, and in Ashdod, there remained. 23 So Joshua took the whole land, according to all that the Lord said unto Moses; and Joshua gave it for an inheritance unto Israel according to their divisions by their tribes. And the land rested from war.

11.13-23 Giants and the spoils of war. In this northern campaign Israel enriches herself with the spoils of war. She spares some cities from burning so she can possess them. The battle conquests are plainly described. This war was a long war (18). There were no peace treaties with any of these northern cities. Gibeon stands alone as the sole city saved by treaty. An interesting note is that the Anakims (giants), were destroyed with the exception of Gaza, Gath and Ashdod. It is from these areas the future battles with giants ensue. And so Joshua took the whole land (23), and the land had rest from war.

Chapter 12

12.1-24 Now these are the kings of the land, which the children of Israel smote, and possessed their land on the other side Jordan toward the rising of the sun, from the river Arnon unto mount Hermon, and all the plain on the east: 2 Sihon king of the Amorites, who dwelt in Heshbon, and ruled from Aroer, which is upon the bank of the river Arnon, and from the middle of the river, and from half Gilead, even unto the river Jabbok, which is the border of the children of Ammon; 3 And from the plain to the sea of Chinneroth on the east, and unto the sea of the plain, even the salt sea on the east, the way to Bethjeshimoth; and from the south, under Ashdothpisgah: 4 And the coast of Og king of Bashan, which was of the remnant of the giants, that dwelt at Ashtaroth and at Edrei, 5 And reigned in mount Hermon, and in Salcah, and in all Bashan, unto the border of the Geshurites and the Maachathites, and half Gilead, the border of Sihon king of Heshbon. 6 Them did Moses the servant of the Lord and the children of Israel smite: and Moses the servant of the Lord gave it for a possession unto the Reubenites, and the Gadites, and the half tribe of Manasseh. 7 And these are the kings of the country which Joshua and the children of Israel smote on this side Jordan on the west, from Baalgad in the valley of Lebanon even unto the mount Halak, that goeth up to Seir; which Joshua gave unto the tribes of Israel for a possession according to their divisions; 8 In the mountains, and in the valleys, and in the plains, and in the springs, and in the wilderness, and in the south country; the Hittites, the Amorites, and the Canaanites, the Perizzites, the Hivites, and the Jebusites: 9 The king of Jericho, one; the king of Ai, which is beside Bethel, one; 10 The king of Jerusalem, one; the king of Hebron, one; 11 The king of Jarmuth, one; the king of Lachish, one; 12 The king of Eglon, one; the king of Gezer, one; 13 The king of Debir, one; the king of Geder, one; 14 The king of Hormah, one; the king of Arad, one; 15 The king of Libnah, one; the king of Adullam, one; 16 The king of Makkedah, one; the king of Bethel, one; 17 The king of Tappuah, one; the king of Hepher, one; 18 The king of Aphek, one; the king of Lasharon, one; 19 The king of Madon, one; the king of Hazor, one; 20 The king of Shimronmeron, one; the king of Achshaph, one; 21 The king of Taanach, one; the king of Megiddo, one; 22 The king of Kedesh, one; the king of Jokneam of Carmel, one; 23 The king of Dor in the coast of Dor, one; the king of the nations of Gilgal, one; 24 The king of Tirzah, one: all the kings thirty and one.

12.1-24 The defeated kings. In the historical account of the wars of Joshua in the south and in the north of Canaan, the only kings mentioned by name are the kings who formed a league against Joshua. In this chapter, all the kings defeated by Moses and Joshua are listed in detail. This chapter is provided to give a complete picture of all the victories, which Israel won, by the guidance and help of God. Thirty-one kingdoms were conquered. This brings the first major section of the book to a close. The Israelites have been given the land and with God's help have destroyed their enemies. The stage is now set for parceling out the land to each tribe for their inheritance. As Israel marched from victory to victory, the Canaanites kept engraving tombstones. The spiritual contrast is immense. To follow God and obey His covenant provides the greatest victories earth will ever see. To oppose God and His plan is to be swept by the besom of destruction.

Chapter 13

13.1-7 Now Joshua was old and stricken in years; and the Lord said unto him, Thou art old and stricken in years, and there remaineth yet very much land to be possessed. 2 This is the land that yet remaineth: all the borders of the Philistines, and all Geshuri, 3 From Sihor, which is before Egypt, even unto the borders of Ekron northward, which is counted to the Canaanite: five lords of the Philistines; the Gazathites, and the Ashdothites, the Eshkalonites, the Gittites, and the Ekronites; also the Avites: 4 From the south, all the land of the Canaanites, and Mearah that is beside the Sidonians unto Aphek, to the borders of the Amorites: 5 And the land of the Giblites, and all Lebanon, toward the sunrising, from Baalgad under mount Hermon unto the entering into Hamath. 6 All the inhabitants of the hill country from Lebanon unto Misrephothmaim, and all the Sidonians, them will I drive out from before the children of Israel: only divide thou it by lot unto the Israelites for an inheritance, as I have commanded thee. 7 Now therefore divide this land for an inheritance unto the nine tribes, and the half tribe of Manasseh,

13.1-7 The tribes on the east side of the river. This chapter takes time to document the inheritance of Manasseh,

Rueben and Gad. The Lord instructs Joshua which land is still not conquered. And how he is to allocate this land. This is the division of the land to the nine and a half tribes on the west side of the river. Some of this land mentioned in the southwest corner that bordered Egypt, was conquered for a brief time but not held by Israel for very long. This land became a troubled area in relation to Israel. It is the area populated by the Philistines, which gave trouble to Israel for many years. This area was the home of the giants of Gath, including Goliath. David did finally wrest this land from the Philistines (1 Chron 18.1), and it became a royal area under Solomon (1 K 2.39). Rehoboam fortified it (2 Chron 11.8) and Joash lost it (2 K 12.18). Uzziah reclaimed it (2 Chron 26.6, Am 6.2). There is no further mention of this area in the scriptures. These passages let us to know there was a back and forth history of this area between Israel and the Philistines. God now instructs Joshua how to proceed with this task just as thoroughly as He did with the physical battle of Jericho.

13.8-33 With whom the Reubenites and the Gadites have received their inheritance, which Moses gave them, beyond Jordan eastward, even as Moses the servant of the Lord gave them; 9 From Aroer, that is upon the bank of the river Arnon, and the city that is in the midst of the river, and all the plain of Medeba unto Dibon; 10 And all the cities of Sihon king of the Amorites, which reigned in Heshbon, unto the border of the children of Ammon; 11 And Gilead, and the border of the Geshurites and Maachathites, and all mount Hermon, and all Bashan unto Salcah; 12 All the kingdom of Og in Bashan, which reigned in Ashtaroth and in Edrei, who remained of the remnant of the giants: for these did Moses smite, and cast them out. 13 Nevertheless the children of Israel expelled not the Geshurites, nor the Maachathites: but

the Geshurites and the Maachathites dwell among the Israelites until this day. 14 Only unto the tribes of Levi he gave none inheritance; the sacrifices of the Lord God of Israel made by fire are their inheritance, as he said unto them. 15 And Moses gave unto the tribe of the children of Reuben inheritance according to their families. 16 And their coast was from Aroer, that is on the bank of the river Arnon, and the city that is in the midst of the river, and all the plain by Medeba; 17 Heshbon, and all her cities that are in the plain; Dibon, and Bamothbaal, and Bethbaalmeon, 18 And Jahaza, and Kedemoth, and Mephaath, 19 And Kirjathaim, and Sibmah, and Zarethshahar in the mount of the valley, 20 And Bethpeor, and Ashdothpisgah, and Bethjeshimoth, 21 And all the cities of the plain, and all the kingdom of Sihon king of the Amorites, which reigned in Heshbon, whom Moses smote with the princes of Midian, Evi, and Rekem, and Zur, and Hur, and Reba, which were dukes of Sihon, dwelling in the country. 22 Balaam also the son of Beor, the soothsayer, did the children of Israel slay with the sword among them that were slain by them. 23 And the border of the children of Reuben was Jordan, and the border thereof. This was the inheritance of the children of Reuben after their families, the cities and the villages thereof. 24 And Moses gave inheritance unto the tribe of Gad, even unto the children of Gad according to their families. 25 And their coast was Jazer, and all the cities of Gilead, and half the land of the children of Ammon, unto Aroer that is before Rabbah; 26 And from Heshbon unto Ramathmizpeh, and Betonim; and from Mahanaim unto the border of Debir; 27 And in the valley, Betharam, and Bethnimrah, and Succoth, and Zaphon, the rest of the kingdom of Sihon king of Heshbon, Jordan and his border, even unto the edge of the sea of Chinnereth on the other side Jordan eastward. 28 This is the inheritance of the children of Gad after their families, the cities, and their villages. 29 And Moses gave inheritance unto the half tribe of Manasseh: and this was the possession of the half tribe of the children of Manasseh by their families. 30 And their coast was from Mahanaim, all Bashan, all the kingdom of Og king of Bashan, and all the towns of Jair, which are in Bashan, threescore cities: 31 And half Gilead, and Ashtaroth, and Edrei, cities of the kingdom of Og in Bashan, were pertaining unto the children of Machir the son of Manasseh, even to the one half of the children of Machir by their families. 32 These are the countries which Moses did distribute for inheritance in the plains of Moab, on the other side Jordan, by Jericho, eastward. 33 But unto the tribe of Levi Moses gave not any inheritance: the Lord God of Israel was their inheritance, as he said unto them.

13.8-33 Rueben, Gad and the half tribe of Manasseh. These lands had already been divided by Moses before he died. This detail is sometimes lost in the overall memory of the land being parceled out to the tribes. The men of these two and a half tribes fought every battle already knowing what they were fighting for. All the other nine and a half tribes fought while being uncertain what they would be inheriting. This section is an appended account of the division of the land and reminder that the tribe of Levi received their inheritance from God, not Joshua or Moses. Two notes: one; the narrative briefly mentions the death of Balaam the soothsayer. Two: the mention of Joshua and his age. The service of Joshua to the nation will now be less strenuous. He will adjudicate in place of fighting wars. Few men in the history of the world have done their work so well. We must pause to wonder why Joshua was not allowed to finish his tasks. The God, who lengthened the day by causing the sun to stand still, could just as easily have caused the age of Joshua to be stayed until he finished the task. Joshua possibly at one time in his life thought he would complete this task while the victories were piling up. Region after region, city after city fell to his army. Every door of this new land seemed to open before him. We are left to wonder why God chose to not use Joshua to the end. One thought is; the enterprise is not Moses' or Joshua's, but it is God's. In God's providence he decided Joshua was done. Joshua had accomplished what God wanted him to accomplish and now it was time to change generations.

Chapter 14

14.1-5 And these are the countries which the children of Israel inherited in the land of Canaan, which Eleazar the priest, and Joshua the son of Nun, and the heads of the fathers of the tribes of the children of Israel, distributed for inheritance to them. 2 By lot was their inheritance, as the Lord commanded by the hand of Moses, for the nine tribes, and for the half tribe. 3 For Moses had given the inheritance of two tribes and an half tribe on the other side Jordan: but unto the Levites he gave none inheritance among them. 4 For the children of Joseph were two tribes, Manasseh and Ephraim: therefore they gave no part unto the Levites in the land, save cities to dwell in, with their suburbs for their cattle and for their substance. 5 As the Lord commanded Moses, so the children of Israel did, and they divided the land.

14.1-5 Inheritance by lot. This method of distributing the land removed potential quarrels, jealousies or strife. God himself assigned the land and God cannot be bribed. God is always fair in his jurisprudence. This is a shadow and type of the inheritance that will be given to the saints of the church age. Ephesians 1.11 promises we obtain an inheritance. God had already stated in Num 26.55 that the method of allocation would be by lot for the children of Israel. This method of decision by lot does not mean chance. It puts the inheritance in the hands of God who makes no mistakes. Prov 16.33 states the disposing of the lot is of the Lord, and 18.18 states the lot causeth the contentions to cease.

14.6-15 Then the children of Judah came unto Joshua in Gilgal: and Caleb the son of Jephunneh the Kenezite said unto him, Thou knowest the thing that the Lord said unto Moses the man of God concerning me and thee in Kadeshbarnea. 7 Forty years old was I when Moses the servant of the Lord sent me from Kadeshbarnea to espy out the land; and I brought him word again as it was in mine heart. 8 Nevertheless my brethren that went up with me made the heart of the people melt: but I wholly followed the Lord my God. 9 And Moses sware on that day, saying, Surely the land whereon thy feet have trodden shall be thine inheritance, and thy children's for ever, because thou hast wholly followed the Lord my God. 10 And now, behold, the Lord hath kept me alive, as he said, these forty and five years, even since the Lord spake this word unto Moses, while the children of Israel wandered in the wilderness: and now, lo, I am this day fourscore and five years old. 11 As yet I am as strong this day as I was in the day that Moses sent me: as my strength was then, even so is my strength now, for war, both to go out, and to come in. 12 Now therefore give me this mountain, whereof the Lord spake in that day; for thou heardest in that day how the Anakims were there, and that the cities were great and fenced: if so be the Lord will be with me, then I shall be able to drive them out, as the Lord said. 13 And Joshua blessed him, and gave unto Caleb the son of Jephunneh Hebron for an inheritance. 14 Hebron therefore became the inheritance of Caleb the son of Jephunneh the Kenezite unto this day, because

that he wholly followed the Lord God of Israel. 15 And the name of Hebron before was Kirjatharba; which Arba was a great man among the Anakims. And the land had rest from war.

14.6-15 Caleb and his mountain. Caleb is one of those people often referred to as "the salt of the earth". Hard working, faithful people who are always there. Dependable in every situation of life, they form the basis for all successful endeavors. These type people are so valuable in a church, a nation, or a family. Caleb reminds Joshua of a forty five year old promise. Forty-five years before he had cut a bunch of grapes from the vine here and in so doing he left a part of his heart in this local. Caleb never forgot and neither did God. Now he is standing before Joshua calling in the redemption of his promise. He is eighty-five years old and facing the giants of the area. There is no reticence or hesitance. His body has grown weaker, his physical physique is aged, but his faith is boundless. His request has become legendary. "Give me this mountain" is as famous as other moments in history that have been hinges of history. This moment occurred at Gilgal where the lots would be cast, and the inheritance would be assigned to each tribe. Hebron is the highest Mountain in the central mountainous region. Caleb brings his request before the process begins to insure he receives the promise. He states "Forty years old was I when Moses the servant of the Lord sent me from Kadeshbarnea to espy out the land; and I brought him word again" (7). Now at eighty-five, he says his strength has not waned. He requests the mountain and the giants, both big things. The details are not given of the conquest of Hebron. We are not privy to the details; we are simply told it became the inheritance of Caleb. We know this: five times in his appeal he mentions the Lord spake. Caleb's faith did not rest in his own ability. His faith was founded on the promise of God. Hebron is the oldest Jewish community in the world. Abraham purchased the field near Hebron where the tomb of the patriarchs is located. Abraham, Isaac, Jacob, Sarah, Rebecca, and Leah were all buried there. This city was where David would be crowned King by Judah, and where David would rule the first seven years as King. Hebron was a city of refuge. It has endured wars with the Roman Empire, and has continued through the Byzantine, Mameluke and the Ottoman periods. The legacy of Caleb's mountain has spanned two millennia. God gave Caleb his mountain.

Chapter 15

15.1-12 This then was the lot of the tribe of the children of Judah by their families; even to the border of Edom the wilderness of Zin southward was the uttermost part of the south coast. 2 And their south border was from the shore of the salt sea, from the bay that looketh southward: 3 And it went out to the south side to Maalehacrabbim, and passed along to Zin, and ascended up on the south side unto Kadeshbarnea, and passed along to Hezron, and went up to Adar, and fetched a compass to Karkaa: 4 From thence it passed toward Azmon, and went out unto the river of Egypt; and the goings out of that coast were at the sea: this shall be your south coast. 5 And the east border was the salt sea, even unto the end of Jordan. And their border in the north quarter was from the bay of the sea at the uttermost part of Jordan: 6 And the border went up to Bethhogla, and passed along by the north of Betharabah; and the border went up to the stone of Bohan the son of Reuben: 7 And the border went up toward Debir from the valley of Achor, and so northward, looking toward Gilgal, that is before the going up to Adummim, which is on the south side of the river: and the border passed toward the waters of Enshemesh, and the goings out thereof were at Enrogel: 8 And the border went up by the valley of the son of

Hinnom unto the south side of the Jebusite; the same is Jerusalem: and the border went up to the top of the mountain that lieth before the valley of Hinnom westward, which is at the end of the valley of the giants northward: 9 And the border was drawn from the top of the hill unto the fountain of the water of Nephtoah, and went out to the cities of mount Ephron; and the border was drawn to Baalah, which is Kirjathjearim: 10 And the border compassed from Baalah westward unto mount Seir, and passed along unto the side of mount Jearim, which is Chesalon, on the north side, and went down to Bethshemesh, and passed on to Timnah: 11 And the border went out unto the side of Ekron northward: and the border was drawn to Shicron, and passed along to mount Baalah, and went out unto Jabneel; and the goings out of the border were at the sea. 12 And the west border was to the great sea, and the coast thereof. This is the coast of the children of Judah round about according to their families.

15.1-12 The borders of Judah. The border between Judah and Benjamin ran just south of Jerusalem. Jerusalem proper lay in the territory of Benjamin. Jerusalem was a border town of sorts between these two tribes until the time of David.

15.13-20 And unto Caleb the son of Jephunneh he gave a part among the children of Judah, according to the commandment of the Lord to Joshua, even the city of Arba the father of Anak, which city is Hebron. 14 And Caleb drove thence the three sons of Anak, Sheshai, and Ahiman, and Talmai, the children of Anak. 15 And he went up thence to the inhabitants of Debir: and the name of Debir before was Kirjathsepher. 16 And Caleb said, He that smiteth Kirjathsepher, and taketh it, to him will I give Achsah my daughter to wife. 17 And Othniel the son of Kenaz, the brother of Caleb, took it: and he gave him Achsah his daughter to wife. 18 And it came to pass, as she came unto him, that she moved him to ask of her father a field: and she lighted off her ass; and Caleb said unto her, What wouldest thou? 19 Who answered, Give me a blessing; for thou hast given me a south land; give me also springs of water. And he gave her the upper springs, and the nether springs. 20 This is the inheritance of the tribe of the children of Judah according to their families.

15.13-20 The providence of God. The inheritance, which fell to Judah, which was Caleb's tribe, included Hebron which had already been promised to Caleb. This was the providence of God so Caleb would not be separated from his tribe. Caleb drove out the giants (14) and then needed to recapture Debir which had already been captured, but must have needed to be captured again (10.38-39). Later the scriptures record Judah went against these giants and slew them (Jud 1.10). It is probable that when the army went north and fought the northern campaign, these giants returned from the towns of the Philistines where they had fled. When the tribe of Judah and Caleb returned, it was necessary to drive them away again. It appears Caleb drove them out, and then later the tribe of Judah finally killed them. Othniel is mentioned here as taking the city and being given the daughter of Caleb to wife. Othniel became the first judge of Israel.

15.21-63 And the uttermost cities of the tribe of the children of Judah toward the coast of Edom southward were Kabzeel, and Eder, and Jagur, 22 And Kinah, and Dimonah, and Adadah, 23 And Kedesh, and Hazor, and Ithnan, 24 Ziph, and Telem, and Bealoth, 25 And Hazor,

Hadattah, and Kerioth, and Hezron, which is Hazor, 26 Amam, and Shema, and Moladah, 27 And Hazargaddah, and Heshmon, and Bethpalet, 28 And Hazarshual, and Beersheba, and Bizjothjah, 29 Baalah, and Iim, and Azem, 30 And Eltolad, and Chesil, and Hormah, 31 And Ziklag, and Madmannah, and Sansannah, 32 And Lebaoth, and Shilhim, and Ain, and Rimmon: all the cities are twenty and nine, with their villages: 33 And in the valley, Eshtaol, and Zoreah, and Ashnah, 34 And Zanoah, and Engannim, Tappuah, and Enam, 35 Jarmuth, and Adullam, Socoh, and Azekah, 36 And Sharaim, and Adithaim, and Gederah, and Gederothaim; fourteen cities with their villages: 37 Zenan, and Hadashah, and Migdalgad, 38 And Dilean, and Mizpeh, and Joktheel, 39 Lachish, and Bozkath, and Eglon, 40 And Cabbon, and Lahmam, and Kithlish, 41 And Gederoth, Bethdagon, and Naamah, and Makkedah; sixteen cities with their villages: 42 Libnah, and Ether, and Ashan, 43 And Jiphtah, and Ashnah, and Nezib, 44 And Keilah, and Achzib, and Mareshah; nine cities with their villages: 45 Ekron, with her towns and her villages: 46 From Ekron even unto the sea, all that lay near Ashdod, with their villages: 47 Ashdod with her towns and her villages, Gaza with her towns and her villages, unto the river of Egypt, and the great sea, and the border thereof: 48 And in the mountains, Shamir, and Jattir, and Socoh, 49 And Dannah, and Kirjathsannah, which is Debir, 50 And Anab, and Eshtemoh, and Anim, 51 And Goshen, and Holon, and Giloh; eleven cities with their villages: 52 Arab, and Dumah, and Eshean, 53 And Janum, and Bethtappuah, and Aphekah, 54 And Humtah, and Kirjatharba, which is Hebron, and Zior; nine cities with their villages: 55 Maon, Carmel, and Ziph, and Juttah, 56 And Jezreel, and Jokdeam, and Zanoah, 57 Cain, Gibeah, and Timnah; ten cities with their villages: 58 Halhul,

Bethzur, and Gedor, 59 And Maarath, and Bethanoth, and Eltekon; six cities with their villages: 60 Kirjathbaal, which is Kirjathjearim, and Rabbah; two cities with their villages: 61 In the wilderness, Betharabah, Middin, and Secacah, 62 And Nibshan, and the city of Salt, and Engedi; six cities with their villages. 63 As for the Jebusites the inhabitants of Jerusalem, the children of Judah could not drive them out; but the Jebusites dwell with the children of Judah at Jerusalem unto this day.

15.21-63 The cities of Judah. This is a list of cities given in the inheritance of Judah. These would seem to be the principal cities of influence. These cities were divided into four districts. Their division was according to their type of land. There was the south, the Negev. There was the lowland, the Shephelah, which was the primary farmland. This is the land Samson would later turn the foxes into and burn down the crops of the Philistines. The third division was the mountains near the Mediterranean Sea. The last area was the desert of Judah. One of the cities listed, Adullam, will figure prominently in the life and journey of David.

Chapter 16

16.1-10 And the lot of the children of Joseph fell from Jordan by Jericho, unto the water of Jericho on the east, to the wilderness that goeth up from Jericho throughout mount Bethel, 2 And goeth out from Bethel to Luz, and passeth along unto the borders of Archi to Ataroth, 3 And goeth down westward to the coast of Japhleti, unto the coast of Bethhoron the nether, and to Gezer; and the goings out thereof are at the sea. 4 So the children of Joseph, Manasseh and Ephraim, took their inheritance. 5 And the border of the children of Ephraim according to their families was thus: even the border of their inheritance on the east side was Atarothaddar, unto Bethhoron the upper; 6 And the border went out toward the sea to Michmethah on the north side; and the border went about eastward unto Taanathshiloh, and passed by it on the east to Janohah; 7 And it went down from Janohah to Ataroth, and to Naarath, and came to Jericho, and went out at Jordan. 8 The border went out from Tappuah westward unto the river Kanah; and the goings out thereof were at the sea. This is the inheritance of the tribe of the children of Ephraim by their families. 9 And the separate cities for the children of Ephraim were among the inheritance of the children of Manasseh, all the cities with their villages. 10 And they drave not out

the Canaanites that dwelt in Gezer: but the Canaanites dwell among the Ephraimites unto this day, and serve under tribute.

16.1-10 Ephraim and Manasseh. The descendants of Joseph drew one lot and divided it. Ephraim took the southern portion and Manasseh took the northern part without clear delineation beside the tribe of Asher. The portion given to Ephraim is given first, and then the half tribe of Manasseh. The other half of the tribe had settled on the east side of the Jordan. Next to Judah, the tribe of Joseph was the most important tribe. It was a double tribe. It was perpetually acknowledged because Joseph kept the nation alive during the famine in Egypt. Without Joseph, the family would have perished. In Gen 48.5, 19, Jacob established these two sons should be prominent and that the younger should rank above the older. This is as it was with Jacob himself and his brother Esau. The double portion of the firstborn remained with Manasseh and consequently Manasseh received inheritance on both sides of the river. In the end Ephraim takes the tribal lead. In Ez 37.16-17 the prophet is told to write upon the stick, and for Joseph, he is told to write Ephraim. It is a sad note this tribe became prideful, and eventually invoked the well-known phrase "Ephraim is a cake not turned" (Hos 7.8). Isaiah said of them they were proud and they were drunkards (28.1). The sad decline of this tribe is indicated with their lackadaisical effort to clear the land of enemies (10). They had the greatest opportunity, as well as the most beautiful land in all of Palestine. They inherited the land Abraham first visited when stepping into the Promised Land. These sons of Joseph did not live up to their opportunity. With the exception of Gideon, who was of the tribe of Manasseh, we watch them fade into obscurity. Nobility of character is not hereditary.

Chapter 17

17.1-2 There was also a lot for the tribe of Manasseh; for he was the firstborn of Joseph; to wit, for Machir the firstborn of Manasseh, the father of Gilead: because he was a man of war, therefore he had Gilead and Bashan. 2 There was also a lot for the rest of the children of Manasseh by their families; for the children of Abiezer, and for the children of Helek, and for the children of Asriel, and for the children of Shechem, and for the children of Hepher, and for the children of Shemida: these were the male children of Manasseh the son of Joseph by their families.

17.1-2 The tribe of Manasseh. Being the firstborn of Joseph, Manasseh received a double portion, one portion on each side of the river. The extra reward was also due to the war record of Gilead and his exploits in battle. This tribe had been part of the group that requested inheritance on the east side of the river. The true Promised Land was from Dan to Beersheba and from the Jordan to the sea. The land east of Jordan was not the promise par excellence. This spiritual dynamic is evident in every generation. Many are content to settle for less than all God promises. Here the rest of the tribe receives the promise inside the Promised Land. This was the land of the patriarchs. It was here

Abraham had been given the promises. Abraham, Isaac and Jacob were buried here along with Joseph's bones. The two and a half tribes east of the Jordan were willing to live in the penumbra of perfect promise. Unfortunately, many people are satisfied living in the penumbra of promise.

17.3-6 But Zelophehad, the son of Hepher, the son of Gilead, the son of Machir, the son of Manasseh, had no sons, but daughters: and these are the names of his daughters, Mahlah, and Noah, Hoglah, Milcah, and Tirzah. 4 And they came near before Eleazar the priest, and before Joshua the son of Nun, and before the princes, saying, The Lord commanded Moses to give us an inheritance among our brethren. Therefore according to the commandment of the Lord he gave them an inheritance among the brethren of their father. 5 And there fell ten portions to Manasseh, beside the land of Gilead and Bashan, which were on the other side Jordan; 6 Because the daughters of Manasseh had an inheritance among his sons: and the rest of Manasseh's sons had the land of Gilead.

17.3-6 Zelophehad. This is an important note in Holy Scripture. Many critics of the Bible attempt to say the Bible does not respect the rights of women. These type statements always disrespect the right of self-will God gave to man at creation. God created man with a self will as opposed to angelic beings. God always respects self-will. This comes to play in many areas of man interacting with man. This affects how God interacts with men concerning slavery, or concubines, or the rights of women in ancient cultures. Just because God did not force man to change these social entities does not mean God approved of them. God worked with these cultures and regulated them as best He could. Here is an example. These women of Manasseh appeal their rights and the true feelings of God toward women are revealed. They are given their rights on an equal with men. This has always been God's attitude toward women. They are equal. This is clearly revealed in the New Testament when men are filled with the Holy Ghost and have the mind of God in them. If you look closely, women like Sarah, Rebekah, Rachel exerted influence and enjoyed the respect due to cultivated women. This was how God felt toward women, while He allowed man to exercise the free will man was created with. This equality is shown even more when there were ten families that received inheritance next to Ephraim, and five of these families were male and five were female. This moment reveals the equality of women in the Old Testament in God's eyes.

17.7-11 And the coast of Manasseh was from Asher to Michmethah, that lieth before Shechem; and the border went along on the right hand unto the inhabitants of Entappuah. 8 Now Manasseh had the land of Tappuah: but Tappuah on the border of Manasseh belonged to the children of Ephraim; 9 And the coast descended unto the river Kanah, southward of the river: these cities of Ephraim are among the cities of Manasseh: the coast of Manasseh also was on the north side of the river, and the outgoings of it were at the sea: 10 Southward it was Ephraim's, and northward it was Manasseh's, and the sea is his border; and they met together in Asher on the north, and in Issachar on the east. 11 And Manasseh had in Issachar and in Asher Bethshean and her towns, and Ibleam and her towns, and the inhabitants of Dor and her towns, and the inhabitants of Endor and her towns, and the inhabitants of Taanach and her towns, and the inhabitants of Megiddo and her towns, even three countries.

17.7-11 Megiddo. Few places in the Bible leap into our modern world with such clarity as Megiddo. In Hebrew the word for Mt. is har. When you add har to Megiddo, your get harmegiddo, which is put into English as Armageddon. The tel at Megiddo is currently being excavated by a team from Tel Avi University. They began in 1994 by exploring in three areas. The areas were early Bronze Age, another at Iron Age, and the third at Byzantine era. Megiddo is of the greatest interest today because of the prophecies attached to it in the future. It has been a place of world turning points in past battles. Two notable battles were when Judah fought Pharaoh Necho and King Josiah was killed (609BC). The second important battle was in WWI when the British General Allenby defeated the army of the Ottoman Empire (1918). It is the place mentioned in Revelation chapter nineteen where the antichrist will be defeated by Jesus Christ.

17.12-18 Yet the children of Manasseh could not drive out the inhabitants of those cities; but the Canaanites would dwell in that land. 13 Yet it came to pass, when the children of Israel were waxen strong, that they put the Canaanites to tribute, but did not utterly drive them out. 14 And the children of Joseph spake unto Joshua, saying, Why hast thou given me but one lot and one portion to inherit, seeing I am a great people, forasmuch as the Lord hath blessed me hitherto? 15 And Joshua answered them, If thou be a great people, then get thee up to the wood country, and cut down for thyself there in the land of the Perizzites and of the giants, if mount Ephraim be too narrow for thee. 16 And the children of Joseph said, The hill is not enough for us: and all the Canaanites that dwell in the land of the valley have chariots of iron, both they who are of Bethshean and her towns, and they who are of the valley of Jezreel. 17 And

Joshua spake unto the house of Joseph, even to Ephraim and to Manasseh, saying, Thou art a great people, and hast great power: thou shalt not have one lot only: 18 But the mountain shall be thine; for it is a wood, and thou shalt cut it down: and the outgoings of it shall be thine: for thou shalt drive out the Canaanites, though they have iron chariots, and though they be strong.

17.12-18 Loss and gain. The loss is that Manasseh failed to drive out the inhabitants of these six cities. The gain was their appeal to Joshua for more territory was granted with a caveat. As the tribe of Manasseh became stronger they were able to put these conquered people to tribute but this meant they were not disposed of. This would come back to bite Manasseh later as it always does. When complete obedience is not achieved, it fosters retaliation in people who have been subjugated. It would seem if Manasseh had the power to force tribute, they could have obeyed the command of Deuteronomy chapter 7 and driven these people out. In the text an anacoluthon occurs as the writer shifts from towns to inhabitants, because the inhabitants could not be driven out. Possibly Joshua foresaw this and therefore granted their request for more land by placing it on a "conquer it and receive it" basis. It seems Joshua was aware of the coming lack of complete obedience, and was trying to get this tribe engaged in complete obedience. In essence Joshua was telling Manasseh, if you can take it, then you own it. No doubt the peculiar history of Joseph in Egypt created this opportunity for Manasseh.

Chapter 18

18.1-9 And the whole congregation of the children of Israel assembled together at Shiloh, and set up the tabernacle of the congregation there. And the land was subdued before them. 2 And there remained among the children of Israel seven tribes, which had not yet received their inheritance. 3 And Joshua said unto the children of Israel, How long are ye slack to go to possess the land, which the Lord God of your fathers hath given you? 4 Give out from among you three men for each tribe: and I will send them, and they shall rise, and go through the land, and describe it according to the inheritance of them; and they shall come again to me. 5 And they shall divide it into seven parts: Judah shall abide in their coast on the south, and the house of Joseph shall abide in their coasts on the north. 6 Ye shall therefore describe the land into seven parts, and bring the description hither to me, that I may cast lots for you here before the Lord our God. 7 But the Levites have no part among you; for the priesthood of the Lord is their inheritance: and Gad, and Reuben, and half the tribe of Manasseh, have received their inheritance beyond Jordan on the east, which Moses the servant of the Lord gave them. 8 And the men arose, and went away: and Joshua charged them that went to describe the land, saying, Go and walk through the land,

and describe it, and come again to me, that I may here cast lots for you before the Lord in Shiloh. 9 And the men went and passed through the land, and described it by cities into seven parts in a book, and came again to Joshua to the host at Shiloh.

18.1-9 Shiloh. The people now assemble at Shiloh. Here is where the decisions will be made for the inheritance of the seven remaining tribes. Shiloh was in the land parceled to Ephraim and was now settled. Shiloh means rest. The war was over; it was time to move into this new land. Joshua requested three men of each tribe to go and sketch the land. The lots would then be cast and the land parceled. The tabernacle was set up. The location was the choice of God and not Joshua (Deut 12.11). This local was not the most accommodating being located on uneven ground. There is a long and storied history with Shiloh. It was spoken of in Gen 49.10. Shiloh was approximately in the center of the tribes, and the tabernacle would remain there for the next three hundred years. It continued there until the time of the judges when the ark was captured in battle in the days of Eli. The tabernacle would then be moved to Nob (1 Sa 21.2). When Saul massacred those people (1 Sam 22.19), the tabernacle was moved to Gibeon (1K 3.4). The tragedy is from the time the tabernacle left Shiloh; Shiloh declined and was eventually rejected by God (Ps 78.60, Jer 7.12, Jer 26.6).

18.10-28 And Joshua cast lots for them in Shiloh before the Lord: and there Joshua divided the land unto the children of Israel according to their divisions. 11 And the lot of the tribe of the children of Benjamin came up according to their families: and the coast of their lot came forth between the children of Judah and the children of Joseph. 12 And their border on the north

side was from Jordan; and the border went up to the side of Jericho on the north side, and went up through the mountains westward; and the goings out thereof were at the wilderness of Bethaven. 13 And the border went over from thence toward Luz, to the side of Luz, which is Bethel, southward; and the border descended to Atarothadar, near the hill that lieth on the south side of the nether Bethhoron. 14 And the border was drawn thence, and compassed the corner of the sea southward, from the hill that lieth before Bethhoron southward; and the goings out thereof were at Kirjathbaal, which is Kirjathjearim, a city of the children of Judah: this was the west quarter. 15 And the south quarter was from the end of Kirjathjearim, and the border went out on the west, and went out to the well of waters of Nephtoah: 16 And the border came down to the end of the mountain that lieth before the valley of the son of Hinnom, and which is in the valley of the giants on the north, and descended to the valley of Hinnom, to the side of Jebusi on the south, and descended to Enrogel, 17 And was drawn from the north, and went forth to Enshemesh, and went forth toward Geliloth, which is over against the going up of Adummim, and descended to the stone of Bohan the son of Reuben, 18 And passed along toward the side over against Arabah northward, and went down unto Arabah: 19 And the border passed along to the side of Bethhoglah northward: and the outgoings of the border were at the north bay of the salt sea at the south end of Jordan: this was the south coast. 20 And Jordan was the border of it on the east side. This was the inheritance of the children of Benjamin, by the coasts thereof round about, according to their families. 21 Now the cities of the tribe of the children of Benjamin according to their families were Jericho, and Bethhoglah, and the valley of Keziz, 22 And Betharabah, and Zemaraim, and

Bethel, 23 And Avim, and Pharah, and Ophrah, 24 And Chepharhaammonai, and Ophni, and Gaba; twelve cities with their villages: 25 Gibeon, and Ramah, and Beeroth, 26 And Mizpeh, and Chephirah, and Mozah, 27 And Rekem, and Irpeel, and Taralah, 28 And Zelah, Eleph, and Jebusi, which is Jerusalem, Gibeath, and Kirjath; fourteen cities with their villages. This is the inheritance of the children of Benjamin according to their families.

18.10-28 Benjamin. Having finished the war, Joshua now sets up the religious place for the nation at Shiloh. With that completed, he begins the final task of casting lots for the remaining seven tribes. Benjamin is drawn first. Benjamin is called little Benjamin (Ps 68.27). The lot for Benjamin is small but very fruitful. It includes Jericho and Jerusalem. It is near the parcel given to Joseph with whom Benjamin shared the same mother. The area had notable cities including Jericho, Gilgal, Mizpah, Bethel, and Jerusalem. This area would become the scene of one of the most tragic events in Israel's history during the time of the judges. It is here Israel fought against each other and 65,000 men were killed over the issue of a concubine. From this small tribe of Benjamin would come Israel's first king and later the world's greatest missionary, the apostle Paul.

Chapter 19

19.1-9 And the second lot came forth to Simeon, even for the tribe of the children of Simeon according to their families: and their inheritance was within the inheritance of the children of Judah. 2 And they had in their inheritance Beersheba, and Sheba, and Moladah, 3 And Hazarshual, and Balah, and Azem, 4 And Eltolad, and Bethul, and Hormah, 5 And Ziklag, and Bethmarcaboth, and Hazarsusah, 6 And Bethlebaoth, and Sharuhen; thirteen cities and their villages: 7 Ain, Remmon, and Ether, and Ashan; four cities and their villages: 8 And all the villages that were round about these cities to Baalathbeer, Ramath of the south. This is the inheritance of the tribe of the children of Simeon according to their families. 9 Out of the portion of the children of Judah was the inheritance of the children of Simeon: for the part of the children of Judah was too much for them: therefore the children of Simeon had their inheritance within the inheritance of them.

19.1-9 Simeon. The inheritance of Simeon fell within the borders of Judah. The land given to Judah at Gilgal was larger than Judah needed. This also fulfilled the prophecy spoken by Jacob back in Gen 49.7. Their inheritance was indeed divided. They received 13-14 towns in the south country, 2 towns in the Negev, and 2 in the Shephelah. These towns had already been listed as belonging to Judah.

19.10-16 And the third lot came up for the children of Zebulun according to their families: and the border of their inheritance was unto Sarid: 11 And their border went up toward the sea, and Maralah, and reached to Dabbasheth, and reached to the river that is before Jokneam; 12 And turned from Sarid eastward toward the sunrising unto the border of Chislothtabor, and then goeth out to Daberath, and goeth up to Japhia, 13 And from thence passeth on along on the east to Gittahhepher, to Ittahkazin, and goeth out to Remmonmethoar to Neah; 14 And the border compasseth it on the north side to Hannathon: and the outgoings thereof are in the valley of Jiphthahel: 15 And Kattath, and Nahallal, and Shimron, and Idalah, and Bethlehem: twelve cities with their villages. 16 This is the inheritance of the children of Zebulun according to their families, these cities with their villages.

19.10-16 Zebulun. The lot for Zebulun fell above the plain of Jezreel. It did not touch either the Mediterranean Sea or the Jordan River, so no water access. It was a fertile broad plain. The prophecy to Zebulun in Gen 49.13 stated, "Zebulun shall dwell at the haven of the sea; and he shall be for an haven of ships". This is not the case when Joshua draws the lot. Later we find their land touched the Sea of Galilee. Deut 33.19 says "They shall call the people unto the mountain; there they shall offer sacrifices of righteousness: for they shall suck of the abundance of the seas, and of treasures hid in the sand." This was fulfilled in the Sea of Galilee.

19.17-23 And the fourth lot came out to Issachar, for the children of Issachar according to their families. 18 And their border was toward Jezreel, and Chesulloth, and Shunem, 19 And Haphraim, and Shihon, and Anaharath, 20 And Rabbith, and Kishion, and Abez, 21 And Remeth, and Engannim, and Enhaddah, and Bethpazzez; 22 And the coast reacheth to Tabor, and Shahazimah, and Bethshemesh; and the outgoings of their border were at Jordan: sixteen cities with their villages. 23 This is the inheritance of the tribe of the children of Issachar according to their families, the cities and their villages.

19.17-23 Issachar. Issachar was given to pursue agriculture and not political power or rule. They are referred to as a strong built ass meaning work and the reward of their labor. Their boundary is noted by cities which would lend to agriculture and crops.

19.24-31 And the fifth lot came out for the tribe of the children of Asher according to their families. 25 And their border was Helkath, and Hali, and Beten, and Achshaph, 26 And Alammelech, and Amad, and Misheal; and reacheth to Carmel westward, and to Shihorlibnath; 27 And turneth toward the sunrising to Bethdagon, and reacheth to Zebulun, and to the valley of Jiphthahel toward the north side of Bethemek, and Neiel, and goeth out to Cabul on the left hand, 28 And Hebron, and Rehob, and Hammon, and Kanah, even unto great Zidon; 29 And then the coast turneth to Ramah, and to the strong city Tyre; and the coast turneth to Hosah; and the outgoings thereof are at the sea from the coast to Achzib: 30 Ummah also, and Aphek, and Rehob: twenty and two cities with their villages. 31 This is the inheritance of the tribe of the children of Asher according to their families, these cities with their villages.

19.24-31 Asher. Asher received as his inheritance the lowlands of Carmel on the Mediterranean as far as the territory of Tyre, one of the most fertile parts of Canaan, abounding in wheat and oil, with which Solomon supplied and household of king Hiram (1Ki 5:11).

19.32-39 The sixth lot came out to the children of Naphtali, even for the children of Naphtali according to their families. 33 And their coast was from Heleph, from Allon to Zaanannim, and Adami, Nekeb, and Jabneel, unto Lakum; and the outgoings thereof were at Jordan: 34 And then the coast turneth westward to Aznothtabor, and goeth out from thence to Hukkok, and reacheth to Zebulun on the south side, and reacheth to Asher on the west side, and to Judah upon Jordan toward the sunrising. 35 And the fenced cities are Ziddim, Zer, and Hammath, Rakkath, and Chinnereth, 36 And Adamah, and Ramah, and Hazor, 37 And Kedesh, and Edrei, and Enhazor, 38 And Iron, and Migdalel, Horem, and Bethanath, and Bethshemesh; nineteen cities with their villages. 39 This is the inheritance of the tribe of the children of Naphtali according to their families, the cities and their villages.

19.32-39 Naphtali. The inheritance of Naphtali fell between Asher and the upper Jordan. It reached northwards to the northern boundary of Canaan, and touched Zebulun and Issachar on the south. Naphtali was to be a hind let loose (Gen 49.21). This is a simile of a warrior swift and skillful. This is seen in the battle under Deborah and Barack where Naphtali excels.

19.40-48 And the seventh lot came out for the tribe of the children of Dan according to their families. 41 And the coast of their inheritance was Zorah, and Eshtaol, and

Irshemesh, 42 And Shaalabbin, and Ajalon, and Jethlah, 43 And Elon, and Thimnathah, and Ekron, 44 And Eltekeh, and Gibbethon, and Baalath, 45 And Jehud, and Beneberak, and Gathrimmon, 46 And Mejarkon, and Rakkon, with the border before Japho. 47 And the coast of the children of Dan went out too little for them: therefore the children of Dan went up to fight against Leshem, and took it, and smote it with the edge of the sword, and possessed it, and dwelt therein, and called Leshem, Dan, after the name of Dan their father. 48 This is the inheritance of the tribe of the children of Dan according to their families, these cities with their villages.

19.40-48 Dan. Dan is a sad case. Originally they are given an excellent portion that was on the fertile shephelah. The land was proportionate to their numbers. For reasons of their own, Dan was not satisfied with this allotment. They later went north and conquered a city called Laish and renamed it Dan after the forebear of their tribe. This was the northernmost point of the tribes, so the phrase from Dan to Beersheba became common to describe the north and south boundaries. Dan introduced idolatry into Israel. When tracing their future in the scriptures they are deleted in all future mentions of the twelve tribes. This is a clear result of a people who were not satisfied with the inheritance God gave them, so they are removed from God's inheritance eternally.

19.49-51 When they had made an end of dividing the land for inheritance by their coasts, the children of Israel gave an inheritance to Joshua the son of Nun among them: 50 According to the word of the Lord they gave him the city which he asked, even Timnathserah in mount Ephraim: and he built the city, and dwelt therein. 51 These are the

inheritances, which Eleazar the priest, and Joshua the son of Nun, and the heads of the fathers of the tribes of the children of Israel, divided for an inheritance by lot in Shiloh before the Lord, at the door of the tabernacle of the congregation. So they made an end of dividing the country.

19.49-51 Joshua. A separate mention is here listed for the land given to Joshua for his faithful service to the nation. The land given was promised by Moses as the land Joshua had trodden with his own feet during the time of spying out the land (14.9). Joshua was the oldest and greatest man in Israel. He did not take any land unto himself, but the people gave it unto him. Joshua waited until everyone else was provided for. He did not receive any of the great parcels of the land. He received an obscure portion of land. This great leader manifested a noble spirit unto the end by his unselfish actions. This is the final tribute to a truly great man of Israel's history. It is also noted Joshua was buried in his inheritance. May all the children of God achieve this simple epitaph; we are buried in the land of our inheritance.

Chapter 20

20.1-9 The Lord also spake unto Joshua, saying, 2 Speak to the children of Israel, saying, Appoint out for you cities of refuge, whereof I spake unto you by the hand of Moses: 3 That the slayer that killeth any person unawares and unwittingly may flee thither: and they shall be your refuge from the avenger of blood. 4 And when he that doth flee unto one of those cities shall stand at the entering of the gate of the city, and shall declare his cause in the ears of the elders of that city, they shall take him into the city unto them, and give him a place, that he may dwell among them. 5 And if the avenger of blood pursue after him, then they shall not deliver the slayer up into his hand; because he smote his neighbour unwittingly, and hated him not beforetime. 6 And he shall dwell in that city, until he stand before the congregation for judgment, and until the death of the high priest that shall be in those days: then shall the slayer return, and come unto his own city, and unto his own house, unto the city from whence he fled. 7 And they appointed Kedesh in Galilee in mount Naphtali, and Shechem in mount Ephraim, and Kirjatharba, which is Hebron, in the mountain of Judah. 8 And on the other side Jordan by Jericho eastward, they assigned Bezer in the wilderness upon the plain out of the tribe of Reuben,

and Ramoth in Gilead out of the tribe of Gad, and Golan in Bashan out of the tribe of Manasseh. 9 These were the cities appointed for all the children of Israel, and for the stranger that sojourneth among them, that whosoever killeth any person at unawares might flee thither, and not die by the hand of the avenger of blood, until he stood before the congregation.

20.1-9 Cities of refuge. The cities here described were the answer for a mistaken killing. If a person killed another individual by accident these cities provided a sanctuary for the one guilty of the killing. It was the duty of the avenger of blood to punish the murderer of his nearest relative. The taking of a human life was sacred in that man is made in the image of God. Shedding of innocent blood is a very sacred issue with God. Therefore these cities were necessary to accommodate those guilty of taking a human life unintentionally. There were six cities chosen, three on each side of the river. The manner was, if a person committed an unintentional homicide, he could flee to the city of refuge. He was to tell his story at the gate and the elders of the city were to decide if he could come into the safety of the city. His story would then be investigated. If the story was as he told it, he was allowed to stay in safety of the city until the death of the High Priest, and then return home without penalty. His penalty was the length of life left in the life of the High Priest. God had promised He would provide a safe place (Ex 21.13). The symbolism was of the coming of Jesus Christ, our High priest. Upon the death of our High Priest, Jesus, the captives would be set free. It is of significance that after Joshua assigned the last parcel of land, the final act was to provide safety for anyone that needed protection. No city of refuge could be far away if it was ever needed. Salvation was to forever be near at hand.

Chapter 21

21.1-3 Then came near the heads of the fathers of the Levites unto Eleazar the priest, and unto Joshua the son of Nun, and unto the heads of the fathers of the tribes of the children of Israel; 2 And they spake unto them at Shiloh in the land of Canaan, saying, The Lord commanded by the hand of Moses to give us cities to dwell in, with the suburbs thereof for our cattle. 3 And the children of Israel gave unto the Levites out of their inheritance, at the commandment of the Lord, these cities and their suburbs.

21.1-3 The Levites. Now that the people had their inheritance, it was time for the tribes to voluntarily give cities unto the Levites who would serve as priests (Num 35.1-8). In this manner the tribe of Levi was favorably treated by being given forty-eight cities, more than any other tribe. These were to be distributed throughout the land so to be able to serve all people universally.

21.4 And the lot came out for the families of the Kohathites: and the children of Aaron the priest, which were of the Levites, had by lot out of the tribe of Judah, and out of the tribe of Simeon, and out of the tribe of Benjamin, thirteen cities.

21.4 Judah, Simeon and Benjamin. These three tribes gave thirteen cities.

21.5 And the rest of the children of Kohath had by lot out of the families of the tribe of Ephraim, and out of the tribe of Dan, and out of the half tribe of Manasseh, ten cities.

21.5 Ephraim, Dan, half tribe of Manasseh. These three tribes gave ten cities.

21.6 And the children of Gershon had by lot out of the families of the tribe of Issachar, and out of the tribe of Asher, and out of the tribe of Naphtali, and out of the half tribe of Manasseh in Bashan, thirteen cities.

21.6 Issachar, Asher, Naphtali. These tribes gave thirteen cities.

21.7 The children of Merari by their families had out of the tribe of Reuben, and out of the tribe of Gad, and out of the tribe of Zebulun, twelve cities.

21.7 Rueben, Gad, Zebulon. These tribes gave twelve cities.

21.8-45 And the children of Israel gave by lot unto the Levites these cities with their suburbs, as the Lord commanded by the hand of Moses. 9 And they gave out of the tribe of the children of Judah, and out of the tribe of the children of Simeon, these cities which are here mentioned by name. 10 Which the children of Aaron, being of the families of the Kohathites, who were of the children of Levi, had: for theirs was the first lot. 11 And they gave them the city of Arba the father of Anak, which city is Hebron, in the hill country of Judah, with the

suburbs thereof round about it. 12 But the fields of the city, and the villages thereof, gave they to Caleb the son of Jephunneh for his possession. 13 Thus they gave to the children of Aaron the priest Hebron with her suburbs, to be a city of refuge for the slayer; and Libnah with her suburbs, 14 And Jattir with her suburbs, and Eshtemoa with her suburbs, 15 And Holon with her suburbs, and Debir with her suburbs, 16 And Ain with her suburbs, and Juttah with her suburbs, and Bethshemesh with her suburbs; nine cities out of those two tribes. 17 And out of the tribe of Benjamin, Gibeon with her suburbs, Geba with her suburbs, 18 Anathoth with her suburbs, and Almon with her suburbs; four cities. 19 All the cities of the children of Aaron, the priests, were thirteen cities with their suburbs. 20 And the families of the children of Kohath, the Levites which remained of the children of Kohath, even they had the cities of their lot out of the tribe of Ephraim. 21 For they gave them Shechem with her suburbs in mount Ephraim, to be a city of refuge for the slayer; and Gezer with her suburbs, 22 And Kibzaim with her suburbs, and Bethhoron with her suburbs; four cities. 23 And out of the tribe of Dan, Eltekeh with her suburbs, Gibbethon with her suburbs, 24 Aijalon with her suburbs, Gathrimmon with her suburbs; four cities. 25 And out of the half tribe of Manasseh, Tanach with her suburbs, and Gathrimmon with her suburbs; two cities. 26 All the cities were ten with their suburbs for the families of the children of Kohath that remained. 27 And unto the children of Gershon, of the families of the Levites, out of the other half tribe of Manasseh they gave Golan in Bashan with her suburbs, to be a city of refuge for the slayer; and Beeshterah with her suburbs; two cities. 28 And out of the tribe of Issachar, Kishon with her suburbs, Dabareh with her suburbs, 29 Jarmuth with her suburbs, Engannim with her suburbs;

four cities. 30 And out of the tribe of Asher, Mishal with her suburbs, Abdon with her suburbs, 31 Helkath with her suburbs, and Rehob with her suburbs; four cities. 32 And out of the tribe of Naphtali, Kedesh in Galilee with her suburbs, to be a city of refuge for the slayer; and Hammothdor with her suburbs, and Kartan with her suburbs; three cities. 33 All the cities of the Gershonites according to their families were thirteen cities with their suburbs. 34 And unto the families of the children of Merari, the rest of the Levites, out of the tribe of Zebulun, Jokneam with her suburbs, and Kartah with her suburbs, 35 Dimnah with her suburbs, Nahalal with her suburbs; four cities. 36 And out of the tribe of Reuben, Bezer with her suburbs, and Jahazah with her suburbs, 37 Kedemoth with her suburbs, and Mephaath with her suburbs; four cities. 38 And out of the tribe of Gad, Ramoth in Gilead with her suburbs, to be a city of refuge for the slayer; and Mahanaim with her suburbs, 39 Heshbon with her suburbs, Jazer with her suburbs; four cities in all. 40 So all the cities for the children of Merari by their families, which were remaining of the families of the Levites, were by their lot twelve cities. 41 All the cities of the Levites within the possession of the children of Israel were forty and eight cities with their suburbs. 42 These cities were every one with their suburbs round about them: thus were all these cities. 43 And the Lord gave unto Israel all the land which he sware to give unto their fathers; and they possessed it, and dwelt therein. 44 And the Lord gave them rest round about, according to all that he sware unto their fathers: and there stood not a man of all their enemies before them; the Lord delivered all their enemies into their hand. 45 There failed not ought of any good thing which the Lord had spoken unto the house of Israel; all came to pass.

21.8- 45 Ministry. This inheritance of the Levite's fulfilled both Gen 49.7 that this tribe was to be scattered in Israel, and Num 35.2 that the Levites were to be given cities by the tribes. In the last census that had been taken, there had been 23,000 males in the tribe of Levi. This suggests that these towns were not wholly given to the Levites, but rather they were given lodging in homes and land for their cattle. If divided equally there would be 657 males for each town. This placed the spiritual men who did the service of God for the nation uniformly around the nation. The analogy here is the ministry of the New Testament. Once the church was established, God ordained men to serve in the New Testament church. In Eph 4.11 Paul records God gave some apostles, some prophets, some evangelists and some pastors and teachers. There is not an exact similitude between the ministers of the Old Covenant and the New Covenant, but there are common attributes. First of all, they were both appointed by the same all wise God. They differ in their ministration but not in their purpose. Their ministration was animal sacrifice in the Old Testament, and baptism and communion in the New Testament. Their purpose under both covenants was the same. They were then, and are now, to serve the people of God in their association with God. The analogy holds true that New Testament ministry is to be located in the neighborhoods with the people they serve. This eliminates from New Testament ministry television ministries, and other ministries that are unavailable if a person needs a minister. God intended for the ministers that serve to be near and available to His children. These New Testament ministers are referred to as shepherds (1 Pet 5.1-4). Jesus Christ is the great shepherd and the local ministers are under shepherds. If a minister is not available for the needs of the people of God in his vicinity, he does not qualify as a true minister of the Gospel.

Chapter 22

22.1-6 Then Joshua called the Reubenites, and the Gadites, and the half tribe of Manasseh, 2 And said unto them, Ye have kept all that Moses the servant of the Lord commanded you, and have obeyed my voice in all that I commanded you: 3 Ye have not left your brethren these many days unto this day, but have kept the charge of the commandment of the Lord your God. 4 And now the Lord your God hath given rest unto your brethren, as he promised them: therefore now return ye, and get you unto your tents, and unto the land of your possession, which Moses the servant of the Lord gave you on the other side Jordan. 5 But take diligent heed to do the commandment and the law, which Moses the servant of the Lord charged you, to love the Lord your God, and to walk in all his ways, and to keep his commandments, and to cleave unto him, and to serve him with all your heart and with all your soul. 6 So Joshua blessed them, and sent them away: and they went unto their tents.

22.1-6 Rueben, Gad and Manasseh. These two and a half tribes had faithfully kept their vows to fight for their brethren until the end of the war of conquest. Joshua commends them, blesses them, gives them a charge to keep the commandments of God, and sends them home.

22.7-9 Now to the one half of the tribe of Manasseh Moses had given possession in Bashan: but unto the other half thereof gave Joshua among their brethren on this side Jordan westward. And when Joshua sent them away also unto their tents, then he blessed them, 8 And he spake unto them, saying, Return with much riches unto your tents, and with very much cattle, with silver, and with gold, and with brass, and with iron, and with very much raiment: divide the spoil of your enemies with your brethren. 9 And the children of Reuben and the children of Gad and the half tribe of Manasseh returned, and departed from the children of Israel out of Shiloh, which is in the land of Canaan, to go unto the country of Gilead, to the land of their possession, whereof they were possessed, according to the word of the Lord by the hand of Moses.

22.7-9 The spoil. The service they had provided to the other tribes was not without reward. They had received equal share of the bounty and were returning home with great riches. They had gained cattle, silver, gold, brass and iron. In addition there were many garments, much raiment.

22.10-20 And when they came unto the borders of Jordan, that are in the land of Canaan, the children of Reuben and the children of Gad and the half tribe of Manasseh built there an altar by Jordan, a great altar to see to. 11 And the children of Israel heard say, Behold, the children of Reuben and the children of Gad and the half tribe of Manasseh have built an altar over against the land of Canaan, in the borders of Jordan, at the passage of the children of Israel. 12 And when the children of Israel heard of it, the whole congregation of the children of Israel gathered themselves together at Shiloh, to go up to war against them. 13 And the children of Israel sent unto the children of Reuben, and to the children of Gad, and to the half tribe of Manasseh, into the land of Gilead, Phinehas the son of Eleazar the priest, 14 And with him ten princes, of each chief house a prince throughout all the tribes of Israel; and each one was an head of the house of their fathers among the thousands of Israel. 15 And they came unto the children of Reuben, and to the children of Gad, and to the half tribe of Manasseh, unto the land of Gilead, and they spake with them, saying, 16 Thus saith the whole congregation of the Lord, What trespass is this that ye have committed against the God of Israel, to turn away this day from following the Lord, in that ye have builded you an altar, that ye might rebel this day against the Lord? 17 Is the iniquity of Peor too little for us, from which we are not cleansed until this day, although there was a plague in the congregation of the Lord, 18 But that ye must turn away this day from following the Lord? and it will be, seeing ye rebel to day against the Lord, that to morrow he will be wroth with the whole congregation of Israel. 19 Notwithstanding, if the land of your possession be unclean, then pass ye over unto the land of the possession of the Lord, wherein the Lord's tabernacle dwelleth, and take possession among us: but rebel not against the Lord, nor rebel against us, in building you an altar beside the altar of the Lord our God. 20 Did not Achan the son of Zerah commit a trespass in the accursed thing, and wrath fell on all the congregation of Israel? and that man perished not alone in his iniquity.

22.10-20 The eastern altar. These partial tribes built an altar nearer to their home and this incited a great response from the other tribes. This posed potential disunity among the tribes. The nation rallied for war at Shiloh to go up against these partial tribes. Phinehas the priest, and ten princes, one for each tribe, are sent to enquire. The partial tribes are accused of a trespass in turning away from the Lord. The fear was a repetition of the incident of Peor (Num 31), and God's anger would be upon all the tribes. They are asked to use the same tabernacle as the other tribes. Again they pose their worry. Achan committed a trespass and the whole nation suffered. The nation had suffered when schism rent the people, and they feared it occurring again. They feared this would happen with this second altar next to the first.

22.21-29 Then the children of Reuben and the children of Gad and the half tribe of Manasseh answered, and said unto the heads of the thousands of Israel, 22 The Lord God of gods, the Lord God of gods, he knoweth, and Israel he shall know; if it be in rebellion, or if in transgression against the Lord, (save us not this day,) 23 That we have built us an altar to turn from following the Lord, or if to offer thereon burnt offering or meat offering, or if to offer peace offerings thereon, let the Lord himself require it; 24 And if we have not rather done it for fear of this thing, saying, In time to come your children might speak unto our children, saying, What have ye to do with the Lord God of Israel? 25 For the Lord hath made Jordan a border between us and you, ye children of Reuben and children of Gad; ye have no part in the Lord: so shall your children make our children cease from fearing the Lord. 26 Therefore we said, Let us now prepare to build us an altar, not for burnt offering, nor for sacrifice: 27 But that it may be a witness between us, and you, and our generations after us, that we might do the service of the Lord before him with our burnt offerings, and with our sacrifices, and with our peace offerings; that your children may not say to our children in time to come, Ye have no part in

the Lord. 28 Therefore said we, that it shall be, when they should so say to us or to our generations in time to come, that we may say again, Behold the pattern of the altar of the Lord, which our fathers made, not for burnt offerings, nor for sacrifices; but it is a witness between us and you. 29 God forbid that we should rebel against the Lord, and turn this day from following the Lord, to build an altar for burnt offerings, for meat offerings, or for sacrifices, beside the altar of the Lord our God that is before his tabernacle.

22.21-29 The answer. The answer provided was for the future children. They were afraid in the future people would exclude their children from the main altar, so they were providing a tandem altar to identify with the same God and same sacrifices. The emissaries were worried they were turning away from God when in truth they were attempting to connect with the mainland for the future generations. This was to be an altar of witness between them and the mainland.

22.30-34 And when Phinehas the priest, and the princes of the congregation and heads of the thousands of Israel which were with him, heard the words that the children of Reuben and the children of Gad and the children of Manasseh spake, it pleased them. 31 And Phinehas the son of Eleazar the priest said unto the children of Reuben, and to the children of Gad, and to the children of Manasseh, This day we perceive that the Lord is among us, because ye have not committed this trespass against the Lord: now ye have delivered the children of Israel out of the hand of the Lord. 32 And Phinehas the son of Eleazar the priest, and the princes, returned from the children of Reuben, and from the children of Gad, out of the land of Gilead, unto the land of Canaan, to the children of Israel, and brought them word again. 33 And the thing pleased the children of Israel; and the children of Israel blessed God, and did not intend to go up against them in battle, to destroy the land wherein the children of Reuben and Gad dwelt. 34 And the children of Reuben and the children of Gad called the altar Ed: for it shall be a witness between us that the Lord is God.

22.30-34 The altar Ed. The misunderstanding now having been resolved the group of emissaries return home with the final knot of misunderstanding resolved. This altar was a witness to their connection to the other tribes as the people of God. The book draws to a conclusion with the nation united for their future.

Chapter 23

23.1-5 And it came to pass a long time after that the Lord had given rest unto Israel from all their enemies round about, that Joshua waxed old and stricken in age. 2 And Joshua called for all Israel, and for their elders, and for their heads, and for their judges, and for their officers, and said unto them, I am old and stricken in age: 3 And ye have seen all that the Lord your God hath done unto all these nations because of you; for the Lord your God is he that hath fought for you. 4 Behold, I have divided unto you by lot these nations that remain, to be an inheritance for your tribes, from Jordan, with all the nations that I have cut off, even unto the great sea westward. 5 And the Lord your God, he shall expel them from before you, and drive them from out of your sight; and ye shall possess their land, as the Lord your God hath promised unto you.

23.1-5 The convocation. After the land was divided, Joshua withdraws to Timnath-Serah on the mountains of Ephraim. Here he spends the last years of his life in the quiet enjoyment of his own inheritance. Joshua then convenes the leaders of the entire nation for his final instructions and warnings before he dies. He follows Moses' pattern (Deut 32,33) in this final address to the nation. This is also done by Jacob (Gen 49), and David (2 Sam 23) in their lifetime. Joshua recounts what God has done for them and the future things God will do for them. He sums up all the great motifs that have been presented in the entire book. He begins by reminding them of the great manifestations of victory they have enjoyed. Joshua exhorts them to keep the commandments of God. If they follow his directives, God will drive out all the remaining adversaries. He passionately tells them to keep themselves uncontaminated by the religious practices of the conquered people.

23.6-10 Be ye therefore very courageous to keep and to do all that is written in the book of the law of Moses, that ye turn not aside therefrom to the right hand or to the left; 7 That ye come not among these nations, these that remain among you; neither make mention of the name of their gods, nor cause to swear by them, neither serve them, nor bow yourselves unto them: 8 But cleave unto the Lord your God, as ye have done unto this day. 9 For the Lord hath driven out from before you great nations and strong: but as for you, no man hath been able to stand before you unto this day. 10 One man of you shall chase a thousand: for the Lord your God, he it is that fighteth for you, as he hath promised you.

23.6-10 Law of Moses. There are many kinds of courage, and it is a special kind of courage to keep God's commandments. Joshua knows it is not always easy to do what is right and encourages the people to keep the law. The danger lies in the association with these surrounding nations. The people had resisted the Gods of the land and had not married the women of the land. Both of these issues would come into play in the future. The admonition from Joshua was to cleave unto the Lord.

23.11-13 Take good heed therefore unto yourselves, that ye love the Lord your God. 12 Else if ye do in any wise go back, and cleave unto the remnant of these nations, even these that remain among you, and shall make marriages with them, and go in unto them, and they to you: 13 Know for a certainty that the Lord your God will no more drive out any of these nations from before you; but they shall be snares and traps unto you, and scourges in your sides, and thorns in your eyes, until ye perish from off this good land which the Lord your God hath given you.

23.11-13 Conditional success. Their future success is based on two things. Number one; their love for God must remain strong. Number two; they must commit to forsaking the nations among whom they would be living. In particular, they must not intermarry with these peoples. Disobedience to God would open the door for snares (net), traps (noose), scourges (piercings), and thorns in their eyes.

23.14-16 And, behold, this day I am going the way of all the earth: and ye know in all your hearts and in all your souls, that not one thing hath failed of all the good things which the Lord your God spake concerning you; all are come to pass unto you, and not one thing hath failed thereof. 15 Therefore it shall come to pass, that as all good things are come upon you, which the Lord your God promised you; so shall the Lord bring upon you all evil things, until he have destroyed you from off this good land which the Lord your God hath given you. 16 When ye have transgressed the covenant of the Lord your God, which he commanded you, and have gone and served other gods, and bowed yourselves to them; then shall the anger of the Lord be kindled

against you, and ye shall perish quickly from off the good land which he hath given unto you.

23.14-16 Death of Joshua. As in his inheritance, so he is in his last comments. Joshua saves himself for last. After chronicling the feats of the nation with God as their helper, and then giving the sagacious warnings of failure, he now turns to himself. The death of great men is never a joyful time. Every person present had lived their entire life with Joshua always there. There had never been a single day when Joshua was not there to lead, to intercede, to be an anchor. Now the time had come for him to die. In this, his swan song, the final gamut Joshua throws down is to beware, do not serve other Gods, or you will kindle the anger of God. It was to be the proverbial whistling in the wind.

Chapter 24

24.1-13 And Joshua gathered all the tribes of Israel to Shechem, and called for the elders of Israel, and for their heads, and for their judges, and for their officers; and they presented themselves before God. 2 And Joshua said unto all the people, Thus saith the Lord God of Israel, Your fathers dwelt on the other side of the flood in old time, even Terah, the father of Abraham, and the father of Nachor: and they served other gods. 3 And I took your father Abraham from the other side of the flood, and led him throughout all the land of Canaan, and multiplied his seed, and gave him Isaac. 4 And I gave unto Isaac Jacob and Esau: and I gave unto Esau mount Seir, to possess it; but Jacob and his children went down into Egypt. 5 I sent Moses also and Aaron, and I plagued Egypt, according to that which I did among them: and afterward I brought you out. 6 And I brought your fathers out of Egypt: and ye came unto the sea; and the Egyptians pursued after your fathers with chariots and horsemen unto the Red sea. 7 And when they cried unto the Lord, he put darkness between you and the Egyptians, and brought the sea upon them, and covered them; and your eyes have seen what I have done in Egypt: and ye dwelt in the wilderness a long season. 8 And I brought you into the land of the Amorites, which dwelt on the other side Jordan; and they fought with you: and I gave them into your hand, that ye might possess their land; and I destroyed them from before you. 9 Then Balak the son of Zippor, king of Moab, arose and warred against Israel, and sent and called Balaam the son of Beor to curse you: 10 But I would not hearken unto Balaam; therefore he blessed you still: so I delivered you out of his hand. 11 And you went over Jordan, and came unto Jericho: and the men of Jericho fought against you, the Amorites, and the Perizzites, and the Canaanites, and the Hittites, and the Girgashites, the Hivites, and the Jebusites; and I delivered them into your hand. 12 And I sent the hornet before you, which drave them out from before you, even the two kings of the Amorites; but not with thy sword, nor with thy bow. 13 And I have given you a land for which ye did not labour, and cities which ye built not, and ye dwell in them; of the vineyards and oliveyards which ye planted not do ye eat.

24.1-13 The official record. The previous chapter and this chapter appear at first glance to be very similar and in some ways they are. The last chapter was the historical view and this chapter is the official review for the future generations. Joshua is challenging the people to (1) put God's word first, (2) live before God faithfully, and (3) to love God supremely. Joshua calls the nation to Shechem where the covenantal history began with Abraham (Gen 12.1-7). Shechem was also a city of refuge (20.7). The covenant began between Abraham and God is to be renewed between the people and God as the last act of Joshua's life. As the official record, this chapter records the preamble (2), the prologue (2-3), covenant stipulations (14-15), covenant ratification (16-25), covenant deposition (26), covenant witnesses (27), and covenant sanctions (19-20 implicit). These things bear the mark of second millennial

BC covenants. This is much like a court document in today's world. In this final act Joshua brings his public ministry to a close. He chooses to do so at the place where Jacob had purged his household of all idols and buried them under the oak tree (Gen 35.2-4). This reinforced the covenant renewal symbolized by Jacob's renewal when Jacob returned to Mesopotamia. This is alluded to in verse 26 when Joshua sets these things under an oak tree as Jacob had also done.

24.14-28 Now therefore fear the Lord, and serve him in sincerity and in truth: and put away the gods which your fathers served on the other side of the flood, and in Egypt; and serve ye the Lord. 15 And if it seem evil unto you to serve the Lord, choose you this day whom ye will serve; whether the gods which your fathers served that were on the other side of the flood, or the gods of the Amorites, in whose land ye dwell: but as for me and my house, we will serve the Lord. 16 And the people answered and said, God forbid that we should forsake the Lord, to serve other gods; 17 For the Lord our God, he it is that brought us up and our fathers out of the land of Egypt, from the house of bondage, and which did those great signs in our sight, and preserved us in all the way wherein we went, and among all the people through whom we passed: 18 And the Lord drave out from before us all the people, even the Amorites which dwelt in the land: therefore will we also serve the Lord; for he is our God. 19 And Joshua said unto the people, Ye cannot serve the Lord: for he is an holy God; he is a jealous God; he will not forgive your transgressions nor your sins. 20 If ye forsake the Lord, and serve strange gods, then he will turn and do you hurt, and consume you, after that he hath done you good. 21 And the people said unto Joshua, Nay;

but we will serve the Lord. 22 And Joshua said unto the people, Ye are witnesses against yourselves that ye have chosen you the Lord, to serve him. And they said, We are witnesses. 23 Now therefore put away, said he, the strange gods which are among you, and incline your heart unto the Lord God of Israel. 24 And the people said unto Joshua, The Lord our God will we serve, and his voice will we obey. 25 So Joshua made a covenant with the people that day, and set them a statute and an ordinance in Shechem. 26 And Joshua wrote these words in the book of the law of God, and took a great stone, and set it up there under an oak, that was by the sanctuary of the Lord. 27 And Joshua said unto all the people, Behold, this stone shall be a witness unto us; for it hath heard all the words of the Lord which he spake unto us: it shall be therefore a witness unto you, lest ye deny your God. 28 So Joshua let the people depart, every man unto his inheritance.

24.14-28 The choice. The people are challenged to make their choice. Joshua declares what his choice is, Joshua will serve the Lord. This powerful moment must have impacted the nation greatly for the scripture records all that generation served the Lord (31). The people willingly affirm they will serve the lord (24). Joshua proclaims them witnesses against themselves. Like an official courtroom document, all this is written down and recorded. So on the spot Abraham had built an altar, and Jacob had purified and renewed the patriarchal covenant, Joshua renews the agreement. There he sets a large stone as a memorial to the nation of their covenantal promises. The long journey that started with the magnificent midnight exodus from Egypt had ended in success. The future was theirs. As they departed for their homes the poignance of the moment must have lingered.

24.29-33 And it came to pass after these things, that Joshua the son of Nun, the servant of the Lord, died, being an hundred and ten years old. 30 And they buried him in the border of his inheritance in Timnathserah, which is in mount Ephraim, on the north side of the hill of Gaash. 31 And Israel served the Lord all the days of Joshua, and all the days of the elders that overlived Joshua, and which had known all the works of the Lord, that he had done for Israel. 32 And the bones of Joseph, which the children of Israel brought up out of Egypt, buried they in Shechem, in a parcel of ground which Jacob bought of the sons of Hamor the father of Shechem for an hundred pieces of silver: and it became the inheritance of the children of Joseph. 33 And Eleazar the son of Aaron died; and they buried him in a hill that pertained to Phinehas his son, which was given him in mount Ephraim.

24.29-33 The death of Joshua and Eleazar. Joshua's long and fruitful life of 110 years was over. He had done all he could to produce fidelity in the nation. Joshua did not formally lay down his position, for he had no successor. The written covenant was to be his successor. This principal was in it's infancy stage and would not become mature for several centuries when the writing prophets would appear. The nation would have to first go through the 450 years of the judges and then the 450 years of the monarchy before the written word would ascend to it's rightful place. In the long transition from the Old Testament to the New Testament, this is the unfolding plan of God. Jesus would succinctly say it to Lucifer on the mount of temptation, when Jesus proclaimed, man shall not live by bread alone but by every word that proceedeth out of the mouth of God. The door closes on the effects of the Egyptian bondage by the mention of the bones of Joseph being buried as Joseph had requested. They had reached the Promised Land. They had defeated the enemy. The miracles and manifestations were written down. The promises were made. It was time for history to turn the page on a new chapter.

The Story Behind the Expository Series

This is a story about a man, his morals, and his ethics. The man's name was Millard Deramus. He was my paternal grandfather.

Millard lived at the end of a dirt and gravel road in Western Central Arkansas. When the road, as it was, reached his homestead, it turned and headed out of the woods. He was born a quarter of a mile from where he lived his entire life. I am not sure if he ever ventured out of the state of Arkansas. Possibly he got as far as a neighboring state once.

Many years ago he had a neighbor he simply referred to as Mr. Poole. One day Mr. Poole left. When it came time to pay the yearly taxes on their property, Mr. Poole had not returned. Millard was a good neighbor, so he did what he felt good neighbors do, he decided Mr. Poole's taxes should be paid so when Mr. Poole returned, he would not be in arrears with the state of Arkansas.

Millard hitched his mules and went on to Mr. Poole's land and cut a load of pulp wood and took it to the mill and sold it. He then went to the county seat and paid Mr. Poole's taxes. The next year Mr. Poole had still not returned, so Millard again cut pulp wood off Mr. Poole's land, sold it, and paid the taxes on Mr. Poole's land. This continued for many, many years. Mr. Poole never returned and each year my grandfather would cut timber off of Mr. Poole's land and sell it and pay the taxes on Mr. Poole's land.

I was there the day the attorney came to see Millard. We were on the back porch that had been screened in, and we were drinking coffee. I still have the two coffee cups we used that day. I heard the conversation from three feet away. The attorney had a briefcase full of papers he wanted Millard to sign.

The attorney informed Millard that according to the state of Arkansas, Millard was the owner of the 280 acres next door by the default of paying the taxes for the last 20 years. The name Millard Deramus was on every yearly receipt for over 20 years. The amount of money being discussed was substantial. I watched my grandfather closely. There was no reaction at all. No smile, not even a raised eyebrow.

Millard patiently waited for the attorney to finish. The attorney requested my grandfather sign the documents accepting ownership of 280 acres that joined his 70 acres. The value of the land at that time, including the timber, was well over a quarter of a million dollars. When the attorney finished and asked my grandfather to sign the documents he quietly and firmly said no, I will not sign. He informed the attorney that was not his land and he had never taken anything that did not belong to him in his life.

The amount of money was staggering to me. I was watching a man who had lived a simple rustic life for all of his eighty-plus years. He wore bib overalls and drove old pick-up trucks. When younger, he worked as a blacksmith out under the oak tree in his yard. I still have items he forged under that old oak tree. I watched that day as the attorney attempted to stoke the fire of avarice in Millard Deramus.

The attorney told Millard all he could do with several hundred thousand dollars. He floated the idea of a new home, a new truck, retirement, travel. Millard just stared at the attorney. No comment. None. The attorney tried again. Will you just sign, Millard? For your children? No comment. None. Finally the attorney asked, "Is there anything I can do to get you to sign these papers?" My grandfather simply shook his head no. He said one sentence. He said, "It ain't my land."

My grandfather died and was buried a short distance from where he lived his entire life. My grandmother (Dolly) lived a few more years. The children convinced her to sign the papers to claim ownership of the land because otherwise it would simply go back to the state. She signed, the land was sold, and my father was one of eight children who inherited.

When my father died I received my inheritance, part of which was the money from the sale of Mr. Poole's land. For a long time I pondered what to do. I did not feel like I could accept money I had witnessed my grandfather refuse on the afternoon on the back porch so many years before. So I waited. I did nothing. I never spent one dime of that money.

In 2016 an idea came to me that seemed an appropriate way to use that money. It is the money being used to produce the Expository Series. I did not know of any Apostolic writings that were doing an Expository Series. So I took that money and began to print books for Apostolic people to read.

The books of the Expository Series are printed without charge to the authors. The proceeds and profit of the books sold online go back into a non-profit fund to print more Apostolic books. None of the online profit is going to any personal use for anyone. If an author buys his book direct from wholesale after it is published and sells it, then he is welcomed to keep any profit from those sales.

I would like to thank all the men who have contributed their work to this endeavor. Scott Hall, Bart Adkins, Vaughn Reece, Kevin Archer, Ben Weeks, and Edward Seabrooks have all contributed. We have now published fifteen volumes and have three more to be published in the next sixty days. Others have also shown interest in publishing their works. Our goal is to have twenty volumes published by the end of 2017.

The publisher we are using has informed me we are their best seller they have ever published. We have now sold several thousand dollars of books since September 1, 2016. I am deeply grateful to everyone who has purchased our product.

Now you know the story behind the Expository Series. A simple Christian man with ethics and morals, opened his heart, and showed me his faith on a warm spring day, in a simple homestead, many years ago. Today I say thank you to my grandfather, Millard Deramus. Thank you for your ethics. Thank you for your morals. Thank you for your Christian faith.

May your memory be blessed and revered. You never travelled 100 miles from where you were born, but your legacy has spanned America.

www.ingramcontent.com/pod-product-compliance
Lightning Source LLC
Chambersburg PA
CBHW071740080526
44588CB00013B/2100